FRANK LLOYD WRIGHT

WRIGHT

A BEGINNER'S GUIDE

FRANK LLOYD WRIGHT

WRIGHT

A BEGINNER'S GUIDE

GEOFF NICHOLSON

Hodder & Stoughton

A MEMBER OF THE HODDER HEADLINE GROUP

Orders: please contact Bookpoint Ltd, 130 Milton Park, Abingdon, Oxon OX14 4SB. Telephone: (44) 01235 827720, Fax: (44) 01235 400554. Lines are open from 9.00–6.00, Monday to Saturday, with a 24-hour message answering service. Email address: orders@bookpoint.co.uk

British Library Cataloguing in Publication Data
A catalogue record for this title is available from The British Library

ISBN 0 340 84614 3

First published 2002
Impression number   10 9 8 7 6 5 4 3 2 1
Year 2007 2006 2005 2004 2003 2002

Cover photo from Bettman/Corbis.
Typeset by Transet Limited, Coventry, England.
Printed in Great Britain for Hodder & Stoughton Educational, a division of Hodder Headline Plc, 338 Euston Road, London NW1 3BH by Cox & Wyman, Reading, Berks.

CONTENTS

Introduction

Frank Lloyd Wright was the first, and perhaps so far the only, truly great American architect.

In the course of his very long career he designed about 1,000 structures, roughly half of which were built during his lifetime. His designs included skyscrapers, schools, churches and synagogues, offices, art galleries, a gas station, a windmill, an auto showroom, a miniature shopping mall, as well as hundreds of private residences. Thanks to the efforts of the Taliesin Foundation some of his designs are still being built today.

There is no single, universal Frank Lloyd Wright style. His earliest efforts, known as Prairie Houses, were built in the suburbs of Chicago in the last years of the nineteenth century. It would be hard to say that they had much in common stylistically with his late structures, such as the Guggenheim Museum in New York or the Marin County Civic Center in San Raphael, California, both built in the 1950s, which in turn have rather little in common with each other. Some of his buildings, such as the Usonian houses, are comparatively modest while others, like the Ennis House in Los Angeles, are extremely grand. While many seem positively minimalist, examples such as the Imperial Hotel in Tokyo were immensely complex and detailed.

ORGANIC ARCHITECTURE

However, what Wright's best buildings do have in common is the matching of form to function. Wright wrote a great deal about the philosophy behind his architecture, yet there is never anything theoretical about his vision. He was a pragmatist. The choice of site was always of paramount importance to Wright and this would dictate the nature of the architecture he created there. His buildings, therefore, attempt to be harmonious within themselves and within their setting.

At their best they look as though they belong, as though they have sprung from the landscape rather than imposed upon it.

This basic idea was at the heart of what Wright called '**organic architecture**'; a set of ideas that he worked on and championed throughout his life, and which are dealt with at greater length later. To be organic for Wright was to be natural and in touch with nature so he used sympathetic local materials in his buildings. He employed local wood and stone, generally leaving them exposed. The internal walls of his home at Taliesin were plastered using sand from the nearby Wisconsin River. The walls at Taliesin West in Arizona were literally constructed from the desert itself.

KEYWORD

Organic architecture: Frank Lloyd Wright's own term for an architecture that was harmonious within its parts and with its environment.

Wright conceived of buildings as a whole. Decoration was kept to a minimum. Furniture was generally custom-made for each project and was often fitted into the fabric of the building itself. On a couple of occasions Wright even designed clothes for his clients to wear when in his buildings. Even if Wright had created only furniture, lamps and stained glass, he would still have been one of the most important designers of the twentieth century.

STANDING OUT

Yet all this talk of harmony and fitting in with the environment might make you think that Wright's buildings were quiet, discreet creations, and they are seldom that. Masterpieces such as Fallingwater, the Unity Chapel, the Johnson Wax Building and the Guggenheim Museum are aggressive, attention-seeking and attention-grabbing buildings. They stop you in your tracks. You have seen nothing quite like them before and you will not see their like anywhere else. They raise the spirits and make you want to cheer.

Wright brings to mind Harold Bloom's point, speaking specifically of literature, that all great art is essentially strange, which of course is not to say that all strange art is necessarily great. But there *is* something strange about Wright's best buildings. They have an irreducible singularity about them. They are genuine one-offs. While some of his buildings blend in with their environment, others look as though they could have been dropped from outer space. They are beautiful and unique, inspiring and unnerving in equal measure.

For all his great international reputation there is something quintessentially American about Frank Lloyd Wright's work, and he built relatively few buildings outside his native country. America is probably the only place in the world where an architect can make his name by building homes for rich individuals and that was, to a large extent, what Wright did.

These residences tend to be ruggedly individual, sometimes eccentric, self-contained and inward-looking, removed from their neighbours. They create a world of their own rather than integrating into the world at large. Even when Wright devised utopian schemes that involved 'affordable' housing for larger numbers of people, such as in his Broadacre City project and his Usonian houses, he still envisaged single homes on substantial plots of land. This strikes me as profoundly, even if not uniquely, American.

Wright frequently quoted the philosopher Lao-Tse and said that a building was not a matter of floors, walls and ceilings, but rather of the space these elements contained. He was also committed to what he called 'the destruction of the box'. At its most basic level this means simply that his interiors tended to be open plan, full of flowing, unrestricted light and space. This has the effect of making his buildings seem much bigger and roomier than they actually are. Wright's work frequently plays tricks with scale. The buildings generally look much bigger and monumental when seen in photographs, than they do in life.

LIFE AND TIMES

Wright lived a long life, full of the very highest drama. He was born in 1867, two years after the assassination of Abraham Lincoln and he died in 1959, just four years before the assassination of John F. Kennedy. By the end of the nineteenth century Wright had already created a substantial body of work. However, the architect Philip Johnson's barbed wisecrack that Wright was the greatest architect of the nineteenth century, seems a long way wide of the mark. If Wright's earliest buildings were literally Victorian, in the sense that they were built when Queen Victoria was on the English throne, the vast majority of his work undertaken in the twentieth century seemed at the time, and still seems now, to be utterly and excitingly modern.

There are always dangers in attaching an artist's work too firmly to his life, but in Wright's case it is unavoidable. When an architect's mistress is murdered in a house he has built for her, the house is destroyed by arson and he then determines to rebuild it, this can hardly be dismissed as mere background biographical information.

When times get hard and the architect's third wife suggests that he write his autobiography and set up an apprenticeship scheme for would-be architects, thereby completely changing his life, his career and the way history perceives him, this too is an area where life and work are impossible to separate.

The fact is, Wright's career was shaped far more profoundly by intense personal events than by any of the great movements of history or society. Perhaps this is inevitable given the high drama and tragedy of his personal life, but one also feels that he was a born egoist. Two world wars made little impression on him; he seemed to regard them as just another example of humankind's idiocy and an unwelcome intrusion on his career. Fads and fashions in art and architecture left him even more unimpressed. He was far too much his own man ever to be part of any school or movement, though he was, of course, more than happy to have followers.

Wright always liked to claim that his genius was unique, *sui generis*, born fully-fledged and not influenced by anyone or anything. This is quite simply untrue. In his buildings we see elements of the **Arts and Crafts movement**, Japanese and **pre-Colombian art** and architecture and even the **International Style**, which Wright professed to hate so much. But these were not just decorative or stylistic flourishes. Wright was able to absorb influences and inspirations at every turn. His genius lay in synthesizing these disparate elements and making them his own.

MEGALOMANIAC?

Wright seems from his very earliest years to have had an aristocratic belief that other people's rules did not apply to him, not in architecture, not in matters of financial prudence, and certainly not in the way he conducted his relationships with his wives, mistresses and family. This led to a number of public scandals and no doubt much private misery, and it may well, at times, have damaged his career. It certainly added to his mystique and notoriety.

> # KEYWORDS
>
> **Arts and Crafts movement:** initially a London-based movement centred on the Arts and Crafts Exhibition Society. It reacted against the dehumanizing effects of late-nineteenth century industrialization, insisting on craftsmanship and truth to materials.
>
> **Pre-Colombian art:** from the civilization in the Americas before the arrival of Columbus.
>
> **International Style:** architectural style that developed in Europe in the 1920s and 1930s. The term was first used in 1932 by Henry-Russell Hitchcock and Philip Johnson. The style is characterized by rectangular forms, open interior spaces, the use of glass, steel and reinforced-concrete, with no decoration.

Wright was the least repentant and least apologetic of men. He believed that anything could be forgiven the creative artist, the man of genius, a man like himself. And how did everyone know that Wright was a genius? Because he kept endlessly telling them so. Architects are scarcely known for their quiet modesty, but even by the standards of the profession, Wright was a flamboyantly arrogant character and self-promoter. He was the Picasso of architecture.

He was a grandly romantic figure, with a large-scale vision of what architecture was and could be. He was charismatic and he knew it. Wright was able to convince clients to do things his way and usually at a cost far higher than they had originally agreed to. And if clients sometimes came away bruised by their encounters with the great man, that was just another manifestation of his genius. It must be said however, that clients also generally ended up with a building they loved passionately.

Inevitably Wright's flamboyant persona did not please everyone and in some ways it may even have obscured his genuine worth. It possibly led some people to believe he was a charlatan, which he assuredly was not. The most extreme adverse reaction to Wright's persona is found in Peter Blake's book *No Place Like Utopia* (Knopf, New York, 1993). The former editor of *Architectural Forum* had had some personal dealings with Wright.

Blake writes, 'In retrospect it is difficult to understand how intelligent, civilized, self-respecting scholars and critics could have accepted this megalomaniac as anything other than an embarrassment. His dress (that of an elderly Shakespearean actor, by the time I met him), his language (pseudo-Whitman), his Weltanschauung (Wagnerian), and his stance vis-à-vis his fellow men and women (ill-concealed contempt) all added up to a fairly embarrassing Portrait of the Artist as a Joke.' (pp.52–3.)

Blake is laying it on a bit thick here and even he is prepared to admit that Wright created some of the most beautiful buildings in the world. He also goes on to describe some hours spent in a comparatively modest house of Wright's that was built in 1908 in Rochester, New York, watching the way the light changed as the day wore on and how it constantly transformed the space in the house.

'This magic that was being performed before our eyes ... was something that could only be generated in the architect's imagination and then translated into reality by various sleights of hand that are not taught in any schools I had ever attended.' (p.54.)

This is surely the standard by which an architect should ultimately be judged.

VISIONARY OR EINGINEER?

Scholars still argue about Frank Lloyd Wright's skills as an engineer. The more indulgent of them fudge the issue by declaring that Wright was simply an architectural visionary. The fact that technology was unable to live up to his vision was unfortunate but not his fault. Tales of leaking roofs in his buildings are legendary. Joel Silver, the current owner of the Storer House in Los Angeles, found that the *walls* leaked because the concrete blocks used in the construction had no seals between them.

Wright famously disagreed with the engineers who were consulting on Fallingwater. The engineers believed that the steel beams in his design, which supported cantilevered decks, were not strong enough for the job. Seventy years later it appears the engineers were right. The house has sagged dramatically and, at present, a multi-million dollar restoration programme is in progress to preserve the structure. The fact remains however that Fallingwater is probably the most beautiful house in the world and the truly amazing thing is that people are quite prepared to spend the millions of dollars needed to preserve it.

Even so, one should resist the idea that Wright was just an impractical dreamer. When the Johnson Wax Building was being designed, the planning authorities could not believe that the slender columns Wright was intending to use to support the roof would be strong enough. Wright famously gave a very public demonstration involving cranes and sand bags that proved his columns could support many times the load he was going to put on them. There was nothing impractical or dream-like about this.

Equally Wright's Imperial Hotel in Tokyo survived what was then the world's worst earthquake in 1923, when much of the city had been razed. In fact the hotel was so well engineered that it was used as a shelter for people whose homes had been destroyed.

Wright was always interested in new technologies. He was a pioneer in the use of concrete, inventing his own building system known as the textile block and he was one of the first to devise various types of heating and cooling systems. His work with coloured art glass was, for many years, state of the art.

To separate the aesthetics and the technology of architecture is clearly misguided, but given Wright's taste for innovation and experimentation, some problems were probably inevitable. The fact remains that Wright's original clients and those who live in his houses today are willing to put up with certain discomforts in order to inhabit an architectural masterpiece. Those of us who simply visit these houses or make use of Wright's public buildings and are overwhelmed by their stature, serenity and beauty, are willing to forgive him just about anything.

✳ ✳ ✳ SUMMARY ✳ ✳ ✳

● No one style encompasses all of Wright's long career but he was always a champion of what he called 'organic architecture'.

● Wright claimed not to be influenced by anyone or anything and yet part of his genius was the ability to synthesize diverse influences.

● Wright is sometimes thought to be an impractical dreamer, yet his works often display advanced technological achievement.

Wright's Early Life

WRIGHT'S CHILDHOOD

Legend has it that Frank Lloyd Wright's mother, Anna, had decided he would be a great architect even before he was born. She put prints of great European cathedrals around her bedroom while she was pregnant and transferred them to the nursery after Frank was born. Since Wright is the propagator of this legend it is as well to be sceptical, but there is no doubt that his mother had high hopes and expectations for him.

Frank Lloyd Wright was born in 1867 in Richland Center, Wisconsin, the first son of Anna and William Wright, although his father already had three children by his late wife. Wright's father, although a cultured and charming man who wrote music and sometimes preached, had a knack for failure and for living beyond his means. He kept changing jobs, moving his family from one city to another, and he never made much money. He was considerably older than his wife, and the marriage was a difficult and unhappy one.

Anna's side of the family were recent Welsh immigrants to America, with the name Lloyd Jones. They were farmers who had settled in Wisconsin at a place called Helena Valley, where young Frank later spent his boyhood summers, resentfully performing backbreaking farm work.

Much is made of the fact that as a boy Wright was encouraged to use the **Froebel kindergarten** educational system, a series of geometric blocks and coloured cardboard shapes that the child uses to make patterns and structures on a squared grid. Scholars have

KEYWORD

Froebel kindergarten: Froebel was a German educator and founder of the kindergarten. He believed in 'self-activity' and play as essential for children's education, the teacher's role was to encourage self-expression rather than rote learning.

shown that reasonable facsimiles of some of Wright's buildings can be made with these blocks. Froebel believed that children should not be allowed to draw freehand. Rather, they had to first master the underlying geometrical forms of the square, circle and triangle.

However, it appears that Wright's mother only discovered Froebel at the Centennial Exposition of 1876 in Philadelphia and so Wright could not have been introduced to the system until he was at least nine years old. It is hard to know what a nine-year-old boy would make of an educational system designed for kindergarten children (his autobiography is confusing and contradictory about the matter), but Wright evidently found it good enough to use again when he had children of his own.

Wright's education was necessarily patchy as the family moved from town to town and he moved from school to school. He had few friends and lived a solitary and lonely existence, taking solace in reading, playing music and operating a small printing press. His parents' unhappy marriage cannot have made things any easier.

In 1884, Wright's parents divorced and Frank never saw his father again. At this point he dropped the middle name he had been born with – Lincoln – and substituted Lloyd, in honour of his mother's family. Since both mother and son believed that Frank Lloyd Wright was destined for greatness, the considerable financial difficulties which now beset them were regarded as only a minor inconvenience, although they certainly had important consequences.

WRIGHT IN CHICAGO

In 1886 Frank Lloyd Wright began to study at the University of Wisconsin. As well as courses in mathematics, French and English, he also studied engineering. This was to be the full extent of Wright's training in architecture and was not so very unusual at the time. He soon left university and headed for Chicago, determined to become a working architect. He may well have been impatient to start his career, but lack of money surely played a big part in his decision to end his formal education.

Chicago, at this time, was an ideal choice for an aspiring architect. The place was booming, becoming a major port, and much of the city had recently been destroyed in a fire. Consequently there was a lot of new building going on and there were many opportunities.

After a brief spell working for the architect Joseph Lyman Silsbee, Wright approached Louis Sullivan, a thriving young architect who designed some of the world's first skyscrapers. Sullivan's company, Adler and Sullivan, was the best-known and most forward-looking practice in Chicago and the natural place for Wright to aim. Wright was taken on and given a job as a draftsman. Eventually he became chief draftsman, in charge of nearly 50 others, and sometimes there was work other than drafting. Sullivan was not very interested in building private houses, so he passed such projects on to Wright.

CATHERINE LEE TOBIN

By 1888 Wright had fallen in love with Catherine Lee Tobin (known as Kitty). She was 16 when Wright met her at a fancy dress party, five years younger than him. Inevitably, she was a naïve and inexperienced young woman and could hardly have imagined what it would mean to be married to a man of Wright's soaring ambition.

Catherine Lee Tobin was also Wright's social superior, and if this was part of the attraction as far as Wright was concerned, the marriage proposal went down very badly with her family. It was received only marginally better by Wright's own mother. Nevertheless, when Kitty was 18 the marriage went ahead.

OAK PARK

The newly married Wright then persuaded Louis Sullivan to give him a five-year contract of employment, as well as a personal loan so that he could build a house for himself. He chose to build in Oak Park, essentially a suburb of Chicago, 16 km to the west, although at that time it was not incorporated into the city.

The area was thriving, growing rapidly, and many homes were being built to provide accommodation for Chicago's newly successful professional class. These people were perhaps not quite so solid and conservative as they might have been in other cities at other times. While they made money and were highly respectable, they also had to be risk-takers and speculators in order to succeed in that tough, pioneering environment.

The residents of Oak Park also had certain aspirations to culture. Concerts and amateur theatrical productions were common, and Oak Park even had its own opera house briefly. These things would have appealed to Wright. More crucially, he may have realized, even then, that his clients and supporters would inevitably come from the progressive rich and he could see the advantage of living among them.

Wright built a house for himself on a desirable lot at the corner of Chicago and Forest Avenues. Today it looks striking, but certainly not **avant-garde**, and it fitted in perfectly well with the other houses in the neighbourhood. It was originally a two-bedroom house with a studio and was subsequently much expanded.

KEYWORD

Avant-garde: literally the vanguard of an army, figuratively the latest wave of experimentation in an art form.

There is something of the grand chalet about that first Wright house. A huge, heavily-roofed gable faces the street. It is clad in wood shingle and contains a row of six windows that let light into what was originally Wright's studio. The ground floor at the front of the house is set back in the shadows beneath this gable, further tucked in behind a wall and hedge. The entrance is a simple door in a bay to the right.

Architectural scholars have discovered that this house looks very much like two houses built in Tuxedo Park, New York by an architect called Bruce Price; surely further evidence that there was nothing very outrageous about the house. Some people claim to see something profoundly Japanese in the house's interior.

Eventually the house would expand to accommodate Wright's six children. The playroom he built for them is stunning; a barrel-vaulted space with a skylight, a brick fireplace, and built-in bookcases and couches. The room was not solely for the use of the children, but nevertheless it is surely one of the most magnificent playrooms ever created.

Building and extending the house and raising children was an expensive business and Wright had already established a pattern of living beyond his means, just like his father before him. To supplement his income he was forced to moonlight and design houses for wealthy clients; not an uncommon practice for a young architect, but one that Wright's contract with Adler and Sullivan strictly forbade. When these illicit activities were discovered his employment with the firm came to an abrupt end.

There is some doubt about whether Wright was fired or whether he left of his own accord, but either way it would clearly have been only a matter of time before a man of Wright's independence and ambition set up his own architectural practice, which in 1893, he now did. Over the next decade and a half, Wright built houses in and around Oak Park, 135 of them, a type that came to be known as the Prairie House.

* * * SUMMARY * * *

- Wright was the child of a troubled marriage and all of his mother's ambitions focused on him.

- He grew up using the Froebel educational system, which seems ideal for an architect.

- With limited formal training in architecture, Wright worked first as a draftsman for Adler and Sullivan and then set up his own practice when his moonlighting activities were discovered.

3 The Prairie Houses

The name Prairie House was invented to describe buildings whose horizontal lines matched the broad, flat landscape of the American Midwest. They were not built in the wide open spaces of the prairie, however, but in the Chicago suburbs. Even though structures such as banks and civic buildings were built in the Prairie style (Wright himself built a mortuary chapel in Belvidere, Illinois that conforms to the general principles), most Prairie architecture took the form of substantial family homes for wealthy clients.

The Prairie School was a loose association of architects based in Chicago, a group that included among others Marion Mohoney, Dwight Perkins, George Maher and William Purcell. Wright was by far the most famous and successful member of the group and would be one of the first to move on. Wright always understood the value of self-promotion and from the beginning he was keen to show his designs to the public. In 1901 he published a design for a 'Prairie town house' and it is significant that this did not appear in an obscure architectural publication, but in the *Ladies' Home Journal*, a magazine with a high circulation.

Wright was also the philosopher of the group and he described the Prairie enterprise in these words, 'In breadth, length, height and weight, these buildings belonged to the prairie just as the human being himself belonged to it with his gift of speed. The term "streamlined" as my own expression was then and there born. As a result, the new buildings were rational: low, swift, and clean, and were studiously adapted to machine methods.' (Quoted in *Frank Lloyd Wright: In the Realm of Ideas*, edited by Bruce Brooks Pfeiffer and Gerald Nordland, Southern Illinois University Press, 1988, p.35.)

In fact it is hard to think of these buildings as truly streamlined, since there often is no curved line in the whole structure, but they do have a sleek, ground-hugging quality. Although there is considerable diversity between Wright's various Prairie Houses, they have a great many features in common. The long low, horizontal lines are emphasized by large, sometimes huge, overhanging roofs. Partly these are practical, to protect the house and its inhabitants from the severe winters and equally severe summers. However, there is surely something symbolic in the size of these roofs, in their ability to act as a shield, to provide a protection for the houses' inhabitants that is more than merely physical.

Nonetheless, the overall effect is never simply horizontal. There are usually plenty of repeated verticals in the windows, French doors and pillars. Set around the houses are porches and verandahs, low walls and plantings, hidden gardens. Materials are 'natural': brick, stone and stucco, wood and glass. These are imposing and appealing houses, but they do not give up their secrets easily. Entrances tend to be small and are frequently concealed. Often what is most remarkable about these houses is what they lack. Wright consciously rejected what he saw as the fussiness of existing houses. He got rid of the basement, the attic and the clustered chimneys that were typical at the time.

Inside the houses Wright had already begun his campaign to open up space and destroy the box-like nature of the Victorian home. There is nothing in the Prairie House that resembles the typical Victorian parlour. Prairie Houses tend to have one of two plans, either cruciform or what is referred to as 'pinwheel' – a series of spaces opening off a central core, which in turn open into each other. Both inevitably lead to an openness. Rather than being a series of self-contained rooms, there are continuous spaces, only partly defined and which flow easily into one another. Instead of being like cubes, the rooms frequently intersect at the corners, creating long diagonal views. Privacy and separate areas are created by using screens where necessary and, as so often with Wright, there is an illusion of scale. These interiors generally look much more spacious than they actually are.

There is very little decoration in the houses; no chintz, no ornamentation. Visual focus comes from the use of architectural elements, rhythmic arrangements of piers and columns. Ceilings within the same room often vary enormously in height. They can be very low in places, while elsewhere they soar up into the roof space, liberated by the removal of the attic.

There was certainly something new and radical about these houses, they were the latest thing, and yet there was nothing bleakly experimental about them. They still provided informal home comforts. There is always a large welcoming fireplace at the core of Wright's Prairie Houses.

THE ROBIE HOUSE
All Wright's Prairie Houses have a great deal to recommend them, but the best, indeed the culmination of the style, is the Robie House in Chicago. It was built in 1907 for Frederick C. Robie, a 30-year-old bicycle manufacturer.

The house was known locally as 'The Battleship', which certainly suggests that it may have been seen as threatening, as well as imposing, and also that the people of Chicago had a healthy scepticism about Wright's architecture. The house is made of gorgeous red Roman brick and it has a huge, cantilevered roof that projects beyond the corners, thereby creating a shaded porch that is entirely protected from the harsh Midwestern elements. There are low walls and terraces around the house, and there is some intentional deception about which are simply garden walls and which are part of the structure of the house.

Although it appears to be a very long, low building it has a surprising height to it, reaching up to three stories. The living accommodation is on the middle floor, which is raised up well above ground level, while sleeping accommodation is above that, with a playroom and billiards room below. There is no basement, of course.

The Robie House

The living and dining rooms are not really separate rooms at all, but part of a continuous space separated only by the imposing brick fireplace and chimney. The space is enhanced with long stretches of French doors, containing Wright-designed art glass. The room is simultaneously alive with detail and yet perfectly tranquil.

Robie was in many ways the ideal Wright client. He was young and progressive, he wanted to reject the fuss of the past and look to the future. It is also worth noting that, according to an interview Robie gave long after the house was completed, relations between client and architect were completely harmonious. Wright's famous extravagance was somehow kept in check. The house was budgeted at $60,000 and Wright completed it for $59,000. 'It was one of the cleanest business deals I ever had,' Robie said.

ARTS AND CRAFTS

It is possible to see a considerable Arts and Crafts influence in Wright's work from these Prairie years. The Arts and Crafts movement was a largely British affair, whose practitioners and supporters included Charles Rennie Mackintosh, William Morris and John Ruskin, all of whom believed that architecture had a vital part to play in the creation of an ideal society. If this idea seems out of favour at the moment, it was one that Wright took seriously throughout his life. Clearly, such high-minded concerns give the architect a huge amount of responsibility, both practical and moral. Wright was certainly happy to take on this responsibility, and the power that went with it.

The area where Wright departed from the Arts and Crafts credo was in his attitude towards the machine. True Arts and Crafts believers would have said that everything in a house had to be hand-made, but Wright tended to believe that machines were acceptable in the making of architecture, provided that they were used well by an able and sensitive architect, like himself.

However, the question of how far Wright was or was not in sympathy with the Arts and Crafts movement is largely academic. Even if one could fit him into the mould and even if he shared many of the movement's tenets, he remained entirely his own man.

It has often been observed that the one talent an architect cannot do without, is the ability to get commissions. This, Wright was able to do from the very beginning. His charismatic personality drew people to him and if being a Wright client was sometimes a bumpy ride, he was nevertheless able to build homes that people liked enormously. Wright was also enough of a professional to give people at least some of what they wanted and this may explain some of his dissatisfaction with the Prairie House. He was occasionally forced to incorporate elements that were more old-fashioned or simply more European than he wanted to. He could envisage a purer form of architecture, more original and something more thoroughly American. Just as importantly, he may justifiably have begun to think that he had exhausted the possibilities of the form. He was ready to move on.

THE LARKIN BUILDING AND THE UNITY CHAPEL

In 1902, while still firmly in his Prairie House period, Wright received his first commission for a large-scale public building. He was asked to design an administrative building for the Larkin Company, a mail order operation in Buffalo. It was a structure that needed to accommodate a staff of 1800, mostly clerks and secretaries, who dealt with the incoming orders. The majority of these employees were female and at least part of Wright's task was to provide clean and pleasant working conditions that would attract workers to what was a particularly grim industrial district of Buffalo.

Evidently it was an occasion when Wright's architecture could neither blend with, nor spring from, the environment and so he created a formidably inward-looking building. The building was demolished in 1950 but plans and photographs show it to have been a large and severe piece of architecture. It was built of brick and it looks slabby and solid, but also very austere. It has something of the fortress and the exotic temple about it, motifs that would figure largely in Wright's later work.

Once you were inside the building, the effect was much less forbidding and you would certainly have felt safe and comfortable there. At its centre was a five-storey rectangular well surrounded by balconies, with stairs at each corner. Inspiring mottoes such as, 'Cooperation, Economy, Industry' and 'Thought, Feeling, Action' were inscribed on the walls of the balconies.

Light came in through a lofty skylight and, although there were windows, these were generally above head height so the workers could not see out. Wright might have argued that there was nothing out there worth looking at and the Larkin employees were much better off absorbing the beauty of his creation.

The furniture was designed by Wright. There were fitted filing cabinets along the walls and metal desks and chairs that were stylish enough to become design classics in their own right. There was a restaurant and a conservatory, and a very early, very basic, air-conditioning system.

The Larkin Building was not especially well-received in its own time, however it was certainly enough of a curiosity that the company was able to conduct daily public tours of Wright's creation. Perhaps surprisingly, its design had a considerable amount in common with Wright's next public commission.

In 1905 the Oak Park Unitarian Church, where Wright was a member of the congregation, burned down. Fires were to play a large and mostly tragic part in Wright's life, but this one gave him a great opportunity. As the local architect, Wright was asked to design the replacement church, which became known as the Unity Temple, though it was first conceived simply as a church.

For all that Wright disliked the box, his Unity Temple is very box-like indeed, again like a fortress and slab-sided. This was partly dictated by Wright's choice of material: concrete. In fact the Unity Temple is the first significant building in America to make use of poured concrete.

There is something monumental about it and again Wright creates a building that looks much bigger than it really is. From the outside it manages to look simultaneously ancient and yet industrial, but the interior is a very different matter. It is simply magnificent.

The interior space feels every bit as cube-shaped as the exterior, it is all repeated straight lines, vertical and horizontal in about equal measure, often emphasized with wood strips and with no sign of a curve in the structure. Some hanging globe-shaped lamps are the only exception.

The congregation is accommodated on three sides and on balconies. This is a layout familiar from Welsh chapels, a means of bringing the people as close as possible to the pulpit. It is also reminiscent of Sir

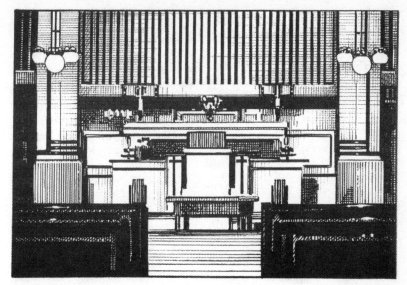

The Unity Temple

Christopher Wren's London churches, built after the Great Fire, where his task, like Wright's, was to accommodate a lot of people in a small space. Wright's interior holds 400 without ever looking cramped.

What makes the space so dazzling, however, is the way that Wright has ensured it is absolutely saturated with light. As with the Larkin Building, there are no windows to look directly out of, but a grid of 25 stained-glass skylights, and **clerestories** around the balconies ensure that light floods down.

KEYWORD

Clerestory: a row of windows, originally found in churches – between the top of a structure's wall and its roof – to allow light into a tall, otherwise poorly illuminated space.

The entrance to this central space is via a run of colonnades and cloisters; one has the profound sense of moving from darkness and restriction into light and space. Furthermore, the main floor is raised up to provide a sense of elevation, almost of floating. It is the most spiritual of spaces.

✳ ✳ ✳ SUMMARY ✳ ✳ ✳

- The term Prairie House refers to long low buildings in keeping with the flat landscape of the American Midwest, where they were built.

- Prairie Houses have an openness and an informality that is the antithesis of the typical Victorian house.

- Having built 135 Prairie Houses, Wright came to feel that he had exhausted the possibilities of the form.

- In this same period he built the Unity Temple, an early masterpiece and the first significant building in America to use poured concrete.

Exile and Return 4

DISSATISFACTION

After the completion of the Larkin Building and the Unity Temple, there were no further large new public commissions on the horizon for Wright and building yet more Prairie Houses had no great appeal. In 1907 he turned 40, and he felt that his reputation was not as great as he deserved.

This was not wholly reasonable of Wright. Very few architects have ever made much of a reputation by that age and Wright had certainly designed and constructed far more buildings than any 40-year-old architect could decently expect. For example, when Mies van der Rohe arrived in New York in 1938, where he was greeted as an architectural god, he was 52 years old and had built precisely 17 buildings. Nevertheless, this would have been no consolation for Wright. He was not a man to measure himself by other people's standards.

An unhappy marriage added to Wright's restlessness and dissatisfaction. For all that Wright frequently appears as a great patriarchal figure, in reality he seems to have found his own children a great burden and a distraction from his career. Allied to this, he resented Kitty for giving their children the attention that he wanted exclusively for himself.

Wright began a relationship with a married woman called Mamah Borthwick Cheney. She was the wife of a successful electrical engineer and Wright had built a Prairie House for the couple in Oak Park in 1904. Mamah was a writer and an early feminist. She had both Bachelor of Arts and Master of Arts degrees and she had ambitions to be a writer. Mamah was a great deal more sophisticated and worldly than Kitty and, even though she had children of her own, she was prepared to neglect them in order to give Wright the undivided attention he craved.

Oak Park was not the sort of place where such an affair could go unnoticed and Wright was extravagantly indiscreet, driving Mamah around in his yellow convertible. Kitty chose to ignore it, perhaps hoping that the affair might blow over, but it did not. Wright soon asked Kitty for a divorce but she refused.

Wright was evidently in great emotional turmoil. In October 1909 he shut down his architectural practice and left for Europe with Mamah Cheney. They both abandoned their families, going into what Wright described as 'voluntary exile'. Their departure caused a very public scandal and Wright's rejected family experienced great financial hardship. This abandonment caused a rift with some of the Wright children that would never quite be healed.

Wright and Mamah were away together for a year, spending time in Germany and Italy. In Berlin, Wright supervized the preparation of a book of his complete works, *Ausgefuhrte Bauten und Entwurfe*, otherwise known as the *Wasmuth Portfolio*, after the publisher Ernst Wasmuth. In Italy, Wright visited Florence, where he began to conceive of building a new house for himself.

Eventually he returned to America, to Oak Park and, ostensibly, to his wife and family. He had left Mamah behind in Europe and he now expressed remorse for the pain that he had caused Kitty and, just as important, he said he wanted to renew his architectural practice. This apparent reconciliation with Kitty must have been largely a sham, since Wright was clearly still attached to Mamah and subsequent events force one to conclude that there was something deeply cynical about his actions.

He began remodelling the family home, converting it into two parts: one part to be rented out to provide income; the other intended for Kitty and the children. This arrangement would, of course, enable him to abandon them once again.

THE BIRTH OF TALIESIN

Wright's mother had recently bought land in Spring Green, Wisconsin; a hillside adjoining some property owned by one of the Lloyd Jones uncles. Wright had already done some building there, the Romeo and Juliet Windmill, built in 1897 for the nearby Hillside Home School, run by two of his aunts. He called the windmill his first piece of 'engineering architecture'. He had then designed new premises for the school itself. The location appealed greatly to Wright for its intrinsic beauty and because of its family association. He borrowed money and began to build.

Originally he pretended the house under construction was to be for his mother, but it soon became apparent that this was to be a house, indeed a 'love nest', for Mamah and himself. It was to be called 'Taliesin'. The word means 'shining brow' in Welsh and was also the name of a legendary Welsh druid-bard who had powers to see into the future. Wright may have seen himself as a latter-day Taliesin, but the name also suited Wright's conception for the house. He planned to build on the brow of the hill rather than on the summit so that, as Wright put it, the building is *of* the hill rather than *on* it.

The Taliesin of today is a vast estate and it was to become an ongoing project for Wright from 1911 until his death. Nonetheless its origins were comparatively modest, certainly in comparison with what it would later become. Early photographs show the main building to have been an elegant but relatively small bungalow, long and low in the Prairie style, built on a stone base with a wide overhanging roof. There was a separate office and drafting room and, across a courtyard, were a garage and servants' quarters.

Wright was working hard to make the house part of the natural environment. The supporting pillars, the fireplace and chimney were made of stone taken from the landscape nearby. The stucco used sand taken from the nearby Wisconsin River. For tragic reasons, however, the original structure did not survive very long.

CHICAGO'S MIDWAY GARDENS

In 1911, with her divorce finalized, Mamah Cheney returned from Europe. Wright, who was still making a show of living with his family in Oak Park, began spending considerable amounts of time in Taliesin with Mamah. A new, now much larger, scandal ensued.

Wright held an ill-advised press conference at which he insisted that ordinary people needed rules but that he, being a genius, did not, a stance that was hardly likely to appease those already outraged by his conduct. A public display of remorse might have done his case much good, but that would have been tantamount to admitting that he had done something wrong; an impossibility for Wright.

Despite receiving a very bad press, Wright now tried to restart his career, with some success. He was commissioned to build Chicago's Midway Gardens, a vast project by anybody's standards. Simultaneously, he began to pursue a commission to build the Imperial Hotel in Tokyo, a process that in 1913 involved him and Mamah spending six months in Japan.

The Midway Gardens were to be a pleasure ground or what we might today call an entertainment complex, in an intensely urban setting with concert halls, ballrooms, bars and restaurants. It occupied a whole city block, with a walled garden at its centre. It was a glorious confection in brick and concrete block, with fierce uprights and futuristic towers and what Wright called 'electric needles'.

The project was ultimately doomed to failure and was demolished in 1929. Not least of the reasons for its demise was the advent of Prohibition. A pleasure ground without alcohol was as unthinkable then as now. Nevertheless, for Wright in 1914, the complexity and difficulty of the Midway Gardens project weighed heavily on him. He was spending nearly all of his time at the site, rarely able to return to Taliesin and Mamah Cheney.

THE DEATH OF MAMAH CHENEY

On 15 August of that year, while Wright's work again kept him in Chicago, Mamah stayed at Taliesin with her two children. Also in the house were various workmen employed by Wright. In the middle of the day everyone was having lunch, served by the handyman, a West Indian called Julian Carlton. It is likely that he and Mamah had had an argument earlier that day, possibly she had even told him to leave, but we shall never know the full story.

After he had served lunch, Carlton obtained gasoline, which he said was needed to clean some carpets, but he had something else in mind. He took the gasoline and poured it all around the outside of the house. He had already bolted all the windows and all but one of the doors. Then he set fire to the gasoline. Taliesin began to burn.

When smoke was seen rising from the estate, neighbours hurried there to do what they could and they did indeed prevent the complete destruction of Wright's creation, but they were too late to help its occupants. When Mamah Cheney and the others became aware of the fire they obviously tried to escape, but as they fled the house, Julian Carlton was waiting for them and he hacked them to death with a machete. Of the nine people who had been in Taliesin that day, seven were killed, including Mamah and her two children.

Wright received a terrible phone call in Chicago and returned to Spring Green by train, to the ruins of Taliesin and of his life. There was nothing to be done for Mamah. She was buried in a grave at the nearby Unity Church and Wright stoically attended the funerals of the other victims.

Julian Carlton, incidentally, had eventually been found hiding in the basement of the house and narrowly escaped being lynched. He was arrested and charged, but he managed to starve himself to death before the trial.

TALIESIN THEN AND NOW

One might wonder how a person could ever recover from the terrible tragedy that beset Frank Lloyd Wright at Taliesin. It would surely have destroyed many people. But Wright could not, or would not, allow himself to be like others. He announced his intention to rebuild.

In fact, the living quarters were the only part of Taliesin that had been completely destroyed. The studio and drafting room where Wright worked remained intact, and he might have taken this as an omen, the triumph of his pure art over the mess of his life. There were others, of course, who thought Wright had been on the receiving end of some divine rough justice.

What Wright then attempted at Taliesin was something far more ambitious than a simple reconstruction. He saw that he had the opportunity, and perhaps felt that he had a duty, to make Taliesin more glorious than it had been before. The initial rebuilding was financed by

Taliesin, Spring Green – Wright's home and studio

Darwin D. Martin, a long-time client and patron of Wright's. He frequently scolded the architect for his extravagance in the remaking of Taliesin, but it appears that Wright had his measure and was able to keep from him the full extent of what he was planning.

Wright intended to create a magnificent and opulent estate, which would also be a laboratory for his architectural ideas and, not least, a monument to himself. There was another fire at Taliesin in 1925, after it was struck by lightning, but by then nothing would stop him. After that second catastrophe, Wright simply carried on building, saying that the third incarnation was the best yet because he had learned so much from the previous two.

While Wright lived, Taliesin would never have been truly 'finished'. The Taliesin we have today is simply what Wright left at the time of his death. If he had lived longer he would undoubtedly have continued to make changes to it. What we are left with is a series of structures, low and rambling, independent but interrelated. They hug the ground, appearing to envelope the hill, to curl around it. As well as new living quarters, there were to be four studios, new guest houses, a theatre, stables and a full set of farm buildings.

It is impossible to get a complete sense of Taliesin from ground level; one needs to see a plan or an aerial view to fully understand the layout. Within the various buildings themselves there are at least 50 rooms, with a total floor area of some $13,450m^2$ (37,000 square feet). However, it also a structure that confounds notions of indoors and outdoors. The gardens form a number of exterior 'rooms', while the interior rooms often open directly onto balconies and terraces. One cannot tell quite where the built environment stops and the natural environment begins. Outside there is a maze of courtyards, flower beds, orchards, terraces, retaining walls and concealed gardens that reach up and down the hillside. Of course the peak of the hill always rises visibly above everything.

Wright diverted streams, planted new orchards and built dams as part of a slightly hare-brained hydro-electric power scheme. Besides constant change, Taliesin also underwent constant expansion. After 1915 it included Wright's aunts' Hillside Home School, along with its land and outbuildings. There was a cottage that had belonged to an uncle and, eventually, there would be a fully functioning farm with a granary, a dairy herd, beef cattle, chicken, hogs and sheep.

Wright was vigorous in buying up pieces of adjoining land as they became available, to protect Taliesin from other people's influence and development. He remodelled the roads to his own satisfaction and ensured the removal of billboards. He also negotiated to have utility lines concealed or buried underground.

In the 1930s and 1940s, Taliesin's development accelerated as it became the home of Wright's apprentices. They would be responsible for turning his plans into reality during their hands-on training in architecture.

Wright's desire for wholeness and harmony reaches its zenith at Taliesin. House, garden, landscape and furnishings all blend together harmoniously. Perhaps all architects aspire to creating a self-enclosed world of their own, and this was certainly Wright's version of that. If that makes Wright sound like a dictator, a visit to Taliesin makes one feel that his dictatorship was essentially and profoundly benevolent.

✳ ✳ ✳ SUMMARY ✳ ✳ ✳

● In 1909 Wright closed down his architectural practice and went to Europe with his mistress Mamah Borthwick Cheney.

● On their return to America he began to build a new house for them, 'Taliesin', named after a Welsh druid-bard.

● In Wright's absence, the caretaker at Taliesin burned down the house and murdered the inhabitants, including Mamah Cheney and her children.

● Wright determined to rebuild Taliesin on the grand scale and this was an ongoing project for the rest of his life.

MIRIAM NOEL

The death of Mamah Borthwick Cheney might have pushed a different kind of man towards a reconciliation with his estranged wife, but this did not happen with Wright. At the end of 1914, he received a letter of condolence from a woman called Maude Miriam Noel, known as Miriam. She had been born in Tennessee into an old and prosperous Southern family. She was a sculptress, had lived in Paris before the start of the First World War, and claimed to have been a friend of Leon Trotsky. She asked to see Wright in order to comfort him. He agreed, and within two weeks she was addressing him (in writing) as 'Lord of My Waking Dreams'. They began a long and tumultuous affair.

The kindest thing anyone ever seems to have said about Miriam Noel is that she was unstable. Less charitable accounts describe her as affected, self-obsessed, self-deluding, hysterical and potentially murderous. She was also a serious morphine addict. Wright's mother, predictably, loathed her. Arguments with Wright would sometimes involve real physical violence, yet they stayed together for eight years.

Wright was initially reluctant to have Miriam stay at Taliesin; the memory of Mamah was still too fresh and, no doubt, he wanted to avoid further scandal and bad publicity. Eventually, however, his resolve broke down and in 1915 he took her there, much to the disapproval of the housekeeper, a woman called Nellie Breen.

Wright, if anyone, should have understood the dangers of disaffected staff. Nevertheless, in October of that year he fired Nellie Breen and she immediately went to the authorities and accused Wright of crimes under the Mann Act. This was a piece of legislation, also known as the White Slave Act, designed to limit prostitution by making it illegal to transport a woman across a state line for 'immoral purposes'. A rigorous interpretation of the act meant that Wright was committing a crime every time he took Miriam from Chicago, Illinois to Spring Green, Wisconsin. The case was thrown out, but later Wright would have further trouble of this sort.

THE IMPERIAL HOTEL, TOKYO

However unsuitable Miriam was as a companion, she evidently provided Wright with some consolation. Wright also seems to have used work as a kind of therapy. Rebuilding Taliesin was certainly part of that process, but he was doing that for himself rather than for a client and it was costing money, rather than making any. Fortunately he still had the Midway Gardens to complete and then came news that his lobbying to get the contract for the Imperial Hotel in Tokyo had succeeded.

Japan was opening up to the West, both commercially and politically, and the Emperor of Japan had personally decreed that there should be a 'western style' hotel in Tokyo; a place where visiting businesspeople and diplomats could find the comforts of home. It was to be built opposite the Imperial Palace and Gardens and it was a high profile, high prestige project. It also guaranteed a number of years of highly paid work for its architect.

In many ways, Wright was the obvious candidate for the job. He had always been interested in things Japanese. He was a collector of Japanese prints and had often put them into clients' houses, one of the very few decorative touches he would allow. He had even been a dealer in prints and had written a book on the subject.

The challenge for Wright was to build something that was not simply western in style and impose it on Tokyo; equally he wanted to avoid creating something that was just a **pastiche** of existing Japanese architecture. Wright described his building as 'not Japanese, certainly, but sympathetic, embodying modern

KEYWORD

Pastiche: literally a medley or jumble, a work of art made up of fragments in the style of another artist.

scientific building ideas by old methods not strange to Japan. No single form was really Japanese but the whole was informed by unity. The growing proportions were suitable to the best Japanese traditions.' (*Architecture and Modern Life*, Harper and Brothers, 1937.)

Although the building was certainly not Japanese, the Imperial Hotel did have a kind of universal exoticism about it. It was a curiosity in Japan, just as it would have been in America. Pre-Colombian or Mayan elements appear in the design, an influence that was later given full expression in Wright's plans for the Hollyhock House in California, a project that he designed largely while he was in Japan.

The Imperial Hotel was by far the biggest project Wright had ever undertaken. He began work in 1914 and it would absorb his time and energies right up until 1922. The building cost $4.5 million and Wright had responsibility for every single aspect, from designing the hotel stationery to making the building earthquake-proof.

The latter problem created major technical difficulties. The hotel was to be built in a known earthquake zone. The site had 2.44 m (8 feet) of topsoil which sat on a deep layer of mud, and these two layers would slide around against each other. There was no way of preventing this movement and so Wright's solution was to accept the nature of the environment and create a floating foundation which would allow further slippage (something he had seen used in Chicago). The walls too had to allow for movement. They were supported and connected by rods in a way that enabled them to move against each other, then return to their original positions.

Water, gas and electrical lines were put in trenches that were separate from the hotel's foundations, so they too would be protected. The roof tiles were made of copper rather than slate, since falling tiles could become lethal in an earthquake. Wright's desire to create a truly safe building seems perfectly understandable after the events at Taliesin. He would not want his architecture to be associated with any more deaths.

In reality, the basic design of the Imperial Hotel had something in common with that of Midway Gardens; a grand overall symmetry and a great many roofs and terraces and towers. It had similarities to Taliesin as well, with its use of multiple courtyards and pools.

Wright made extensive use of a decorative lava stone called oya. This amazing substance was soft and wet when first quarried, having a consistency somewhat like hard cheese. It could be carved while in this state, but it hardened as it dried out. The effect looks extraordinary, as though the walls were carved out of living rock.

In 1923 the expected earthquake came. To Wright's evident pride and satisfaction the Imperial Hotel remained safely intact. According to his own account, not a single pane of glass was broken. Although it was by no means the only building left standing (Wright would sometimes claim this was the case), it was certainly one of the biggest and most impressive to survive in the ruined city. Wright was even more pleased when he heard that hundreds of homeless survivors had flocked to his creation for shelter, largely because the water and electricity supplies were still working.

The hotel was occupied by the United States Army after the Second World War and Wright was given the opportunity to remodel it. However, this was one project he chose not to revisit. It does seem that a change came over Wright while he was in Tokyo. There are those who say that his heart was not really in the Imperial Hotel, that he regarded it as a problem to be solved, rather than as something he really believed in. It is surely significant that, even though he would later have plans to build in Venice and Baghdad, once the Imperial Hotel was completed Wright never undertook another commission outside the United States.

WRIGHT IN CALIFORNIA

While in Japan, Wright designed Hollyhock House for Louise Aline Barnsdall, the heiress to an oil fortune and the owner of 14.5 hectares (36 acres) of land in Hollywood, called Olive Hill. She envisaged an artists' colony there; a self-contained community with studios, a theatre and living quarters for artists. Hollyhock House was to be her own home and the centre piece.

Aline Barnsdall was typical of a certain kind of Frank Lloyd Wright client: bohemian, high-minded, simultaneously rich and unworldly. She championed liberal causes and avant-garde art and was enough of an outsider to think nothing of having had a child out of wedlock. She and Wright found each other to be kindred spirits and, over the years, she commissioned a considerable number of buildings from him, very few of which were actually built.

Their relationship eventually soured. Aline Barnsdall was too restless to ever fully enjoy the house that Wright built for her, so in 1927 she gave the estate to the city of Los Angeles, for use as a public art park. The experience was even bad enough to turn Wright against his creation. For many years Hollyhock House was seen as an aberration by an architect who was still best known for his Prairie Houses.

Hollyhock House, Los Angeles

Today, however, there are those who consider it one of the great buildings of the twentieth century and Hollyhock House is one of the 17 Frank Lloyd Wright buildings designated by the American Institute of Architects to be maintained as a monument to American culture.

Certainly it is different from anything Wright had built before, although a house he built in Ashiya, Japan at much the same time has some superficial resemblances. Hollyhock House is, then, a transitional work, and it represents a boldness, freshness and confidence that is rare, even by Wright's standards.

The face that Hollyhock House initially presents to the world is forbidding and fortress-like, with huge windowless walls. Henry-Russell Hitchcock, who wrote a book about Wright in 1942, stated that the house was constructed from poured concrete and, presumably, Wright was happy for him to believe that. We now know that it was built out of a wooden frame, faced with stucco. Hitchcock could be forgiven for making such a mistake, the house appears to have a formidable solidity and weight.

Hollyhock House is usually described as looking like a Mayan temple, but some people have detected Egyptian and indeed Japanese influences. Wright himself called the style 'California Romanza' – a musical term meaning to have the freedom to create one's own form.

As with other Wright buildings, the imposing first impression gives way to something more welcoming, an inner world with courtyards and bridges, obscure corners and tranquil shallow pools. Inside the house itself, the main living-room has a spectacularly high ceiling with a skylight and at the heart of the room is another of Wright's vast, yet reassuring, cast stone fireplaces that has a water feature in the hearth.

The house derives its name from Aline Barnsdall's favourite flower and Wright incorporated an abstract version of the hollyhock into the fabric of the building, as well as into some of the furniture, especially the magnificent dining chairs, but even a keen gardener might be forgiven for not recognizing the motif.

There is something deeply theatrical and perhaps a little over-dramatic about Hollyhock House and in that sense it could be said to be a very appropriate structure for Hollywood. It looks like a movie set and one could imagine all sorts of mythical, elemental dramas being enacted there. To that extent, Wright understood California and its inhabitants very well.

California and especially Los Angeles were places of obvious appeal for Wright. They still had something of the booming new frontier about them. The inhabitants were progressive, willing to take chances, and some of them were very wealthy. As with Chicago at the start of Wright's career, there were plenty of opportunities for architects.

Moreover, Wright's daughter Catherine and his son Lloyd were already in California. Lloyd had moved there and set himself up as an independent draftsman, but by 1916 he was head of the design department at Paramount Studios. He worked with his father on Hollyhock House and on subsequent projects, although it was a predictably fraught relationship.

Wright was sufficiently attracted to Los Angeles to move there in 1923. The stay was brief, but it produced some of his most spectacular and original designs.

THE TEXTILE BLOCK HOUSES

Hollyhock House had taken a comparatively long time to build. The earliest drawings date from 1913 (although this would have been before Aline Barnsdall even bought the land), and Wright was still working for Aline Barnsdall in 1921. However, after arriving in California, Wright produced four magnificent residences in just two years. These are the four 'textile block' houses: The Millard House (known as La Miniatura), The Freeman House, the Storer House and the Ennis House.

The term 'textile block' is a more elegant word for what is essentially the concrete slab. Wright had long experimented with concrete. It was ostensibly a crude, unyielding and unattractive material and he took a delight in creating beautiful buildings out of something that many people would have considered ugly and worthless.

KEYWORD

Textile block: Wright's own term for a concrete slab, created on site, imprinted with a pattern.

Wright wrote in his autobiography, 'We would take that despised outcast of the building industry – the concrete block – out from underfoot or from the gutter – find a hitherto unsuspected soul in it – make it live as a thing of beauty – textured like the trees. Yes, the building would be made of "blocks" as a kind of tree itself standing at home among the other trees in its own native land.' In fact La Miniatura seems the least tree-like of buildings, rather it is a dense, weighty mass, but certainly it looks more alive, indeed organic, than most concrete structures one has ever seen.

The textile block method was intended to be cheap and easy. In fact, Wright briefly envisaged it as a means of creating mass-produced housing, an idea he would come to again later. The blocks were to be cast on site, in moulds that created a repeated geometrical pattern on the concrete surface. Once cast they could be used like a series of building blocks. They were connected to each other and held in place by steel rods, often around hollow cores that housed ventilation and service systems.

Unfortunately, the method was not nearly as easy as it sounded. For one thing Wright's designs required an enormous number of blocks. Even the Freeman House, which was the smallest of the four, used 11,000. Casting that quantity on site created serious logistical problems. Despite the grid-like system of construction and although all the blocks looked superficially very similar to each other, in reality many different sized and shaped blocks had to be cast in order to create the effect Wright was looking for. Things became even more complicated when some of the blocks had to be cast more than once before the pattern would hold on their surface. They could also take a very long time to dry.

Nonetheless, if the means was not as quick or straightforward as Wright had hoped, the end result was more than worth the trouble. In the finished houses the blocks create rhythm and repetition and there is variation too. These buildings look supremely well ordered and yet their surfaces look alive and organic, like something woven. Walls undulate and some of them are pierced so that light penetrates. There is not the slightest doubt that these buildings are made of concrete, you could not mistake it for anything else, yet they have a simultaneous density and lightness.

The Ennis House

Land was expensive in Los Angeles, even in the 1920s, and space was at a premium. All four textile block houses were built on hillsides, in conditions utterly unlike the wide open spaces that Wright was familiar with in the Midwest. He had to break one of his own rules in the case of the Storer House and build on the very top of a hill.

As ever, Wright played tricks with scale. Photographs of these buildings give almost no sense of their actual size. Although La Miniatura is indeed small it looks extremely substantial. The Freeman House, which is probably the most beautiful of the four, can be found on a suburban street in the Hollywood Hills. In terms of its size it is no grander than any of its modest neighbours.

There is something perfect and irreducible about these textile block houses. If all the rest of Wright's work were suddenly to disappear, these would be enough to prove his genius. They embody all of his virtues. They are significant without being pompous, monumental yet light.

The living-room of the Freeman House is one of Wright's most magnificent spaces. Standing in it, you look out across Los Angeles, through French doors and large corner windows that are '**butt-glazed**' (i.e. they have no corner mullion so that the edges of the room disappear and become part of the space beyond). To be in that room is to feel like you are riding a flying carpet across the city.

> ## KEYWORD
>
> Butt-glazed: corner windows that abut each other without a mullion; part of Wright's desire to destroy the box-like nature of rooms.

❋ ❋ ❋ SUMMARY ❋ ❋ ❋

● After the Taliesin tragedy, Wright threw himself into his work and into a bad relationship with Miriam Noel.

● He completed the Imperial Hotel in Tokyo, a vast project designed to withstand an earthquake, which it did successfully in 1923.

● Wright moved briefly to California and produced four 'textile block' houses, using a prefabricated concrete system. These are some of his best and most extraordinary works.

The Lean Years

1923 was the year that Wright's beloved mother died and also the year that Kitty finally agreed to give him a divorce. Consequently he married Miriam Noel. Their relationship continued to be as stormy as ever and perhaps Wright hoped that being married would result in a more placid life. This was a vain hope. However, marriage was apparently what was needed to bring the relationship to a head. After six months of marriage, Miriam left Taliesin and Wright, never to return. Her parting remark was that she would never let another woman have him and she tried very hard to be as good as her word.

Wright was evidently a man who could not do without a female companion. Almost immediately he began a relationship with Olgivanna Ivanovna Lazovich Hinzenberg, the daughter of a Montenegrin judge, a follower of the Russian mystic Gurdjieff, and at the age of 26, 32 years Wright's junior.

Much like Miriam Noel, Olgivanna had led a colourful and romantic life. She spoke several languages, had lived in Russia and, at the age of 18 had married a Russian architect, Vlademar Hinzenberg. She always said their marriage had been loveless, although there was one daughter, Svetlana. Olgivanna was awaiting a divorce when she first met Wright.

It was to be by far the most important, sustained and happy relationship of Wright's life. At last he had met someone as strong and complicated as himself, someone who believed in his genius as much as he did. From then on, Olgivanna was to become a vital part of his life, his supporter and champion until his death and then the guardian of his posthumous reputation.

She moved into Taliesin and was soon pregnant by Wright. This led to a new scandal, at least partly stoked by Miriam who was infuriated by these developments. For the next few years Miriam campaigned to destroy Wright. She went to his bankers and creditors and had considerable success in damaging his professional reputation. It had always required feats of financial ingenuity to keep Wright solvent, based on a general confidence that he would eventually be good for his debts. Miriam did her best to destroy that confidence.

Miriam also stalked the couple, broke into their house, threatened to shoot them, threw lawsuits at them – Olgivanna's immigrant status was always dubious – and she pursued them around the country. To be fair, Olgivanna's husband was pursuing them as well, though in a much less manic and vengeful way.

Eventually Wright and Olgivanna fled to a cottage in Minnesota and this time, at Miriam's instigation, Wright was indeed arrested under the terms of the Mann Act. He had taken Olgivanna across a state line for purposes that the local sheriff considered immoral.

Although the charges were again eventually dropped, this new scandal was immensely harmful to Wright's career. He obviously made a habit of this kind of thing. He was now regarded as a disreputable scoundrel, a despoiler of women, morally as well as financially bankrupt. Few wanted to employ such an architect. His career went into a serious lull.

In 1925, incredibly, Taliesin burned down again. Wright took out more loans and began to rebuild, but the bank foreclosed on his mortgage and in 1926 the Bank of Wisconsin briefly took the title deeds to Taliesin. Wright had to be bailed out by friends once more. In 1927 Miriam finally divorced him and they came to financial settlement, but Wright was so penniless that his friends had to club together to pay Miriam's alimony.

The 1920s were a boom time for America, but not for Wright. Commissions were thin on the ground. In 1928, somewhat out of the blue, he received a commission for the Arizona Biltmore Hotel in Phoenix, a speculative luxury development financed by two brothers who owned a car dealership.

It was a very difficult project. Building in the Arizona desert created brand new problems that Wright had never encountered before and this was to be another textile block construction, this time requiring 250,000 blocks. Wright was also working on another Arizona project called San Marcos-in-the-Desert, a luxury resort to be built near the town of Chandler. This was never built, but these two experiments with desert architecture would have enormous significance for Wright.

Then in 1929 came the Great Crash. If Wright had found it difficult to get work during a boom, how could he possibly expect to get any in a depression? Wright was considered a disreputable has-been. He was 62 years old and his future looked utterly bleak.

Until the end of 1929, Miriam Noel was still bringing legal actions against Wright. By then he was not taking them very seriously, perhaps because there was little else she could do to him. He then learned that she was in hospital and did not have very long to live. She died in January 1930 and, although he did not attend her funeral, when her estate was settled Wright received $5000, money that he desperately needed.

THE TALIESIN FOUNDATION

If Wright's career was in crisis, at least his private life was happy and stable. He and Olgivanna were still together and in 1928 they married. Olgivanna still had complete faith in Wright and his genius. Under her guidance he decided that if he could not practise architecture he should at least lecture and write about it.

In 1927 Wright began a series of articles entitled 'Under the Cause of Architecture' which were published in the *Architectural Record*. In 1930 he gave a series of lectures at Princeton University that became a book called *Modern Architecture*. These activities kept him in the public eye, as did an exhibition of his work that toured internationally, visiting New York, Amsterdam, Berlin and Brussels, among other places.

There was still great curiosity about Wright's life and work, some of it prurient no doubt, and Olgivanna encouraged him to write his autobiography. This was a brilliant and very effective idea. All autobiographies involve a certain amount of reinvention and Wright had never been averse to self-mythologizing and self-aggrandizement. Now he was able to reinvent himself anew and tell the world of his genius.

Today, Wright's *Autobiography*, which was eventually published in 1932, seems a rather florid and overwrought affair, full of improbable-sounding stories, self-justification and far too many purple passages. Nevertheless, at the time it was well received, it sold very well and did Wright a world of good.

In this extract from the book, he is talking about leaving Kitty and the children, 'So, when family-life in Oak Park in that spring of 1909, conspired against the freedom to which I had come to feel every soul entitled and I had no choice would I keep my self-respect, but to go out, a voluntary exile, into the uncharted and unknown deprived of legal protection to get my back against the wall and live, if I could, an unconventional life – then I turned to the hill in the Valley as my Grandfather before me had turned to America – as a hope and haven – forgetful for the time being of grandfathers' "Isaiah." Smiting and punishment.'

At around this time, Wright and Olgivanna also came up with the idea of creating the Taliesin Fellowship, an educational programme under which apprentices would essentially pay to work on the Taliesin estate. The yearly tuition fee was $650.

The plan may have had a whiff of desperation – those who can, do; those who can't, teach – but it made good financial sense. If enough apprentices could be recruited, then both Wright's and Taliesin's future would be a great deal more secure. And there was no doubt that Wright had a lot to teach.

The original conception of the Taliesin Fellowship was comparatively workaday. Wright envisaged a combination of hard manual labour along with sessions at the drafting table, though rather less of the latter than the former. Only gradually did more philosophical and spiritual concerns become part of the plan and this was largely Olgivanna's doing, based on her experiences with the mystic, Gurdjieff.

There was little formal architectural training – not so surprising since Wright himself had had none – but working alongside the great man was supposed to be an inspiration and, to be fair to Wright, many found that it was. Also, because of the depression, Wright was able to recruit the occasional struggling young architect or engineer who found a stay at Taliesin a temporary solution to his own economic troubles.

There was an idealism and a naïvety about the Taliesin Fellowship that is hard to comprehend today. The routines of unpaid labour and communal living, interspersed with picnics, choral practices and concert parties certainly have their comical side. The apprentices were subject to the whims of both Wright and Olgivanna, which extended to matters of diet and dress. Expulsions for sexual misbehaviour were not uncommon.

Accounts of Taliesin at this time describe it as a chaotic place, full of half-finished projects and the young apprentices struggling with machines they did not know how to use. However, they did get to create architecture work with Frank Lloyd Wright. The fact that Wright could hold such a group together is some indication of the strength of his character, and he did spark a great loyalty in many of his apprentices, some of whom went on to be architects, others who went on to become clients.

No doubt Wright felt beleaguered at this time. The commissions were still not coming in, but he could at least console himself with the knowledge that he now had disciples and that he was perhaps a prophet in the wilderness. If he felt abused he certainly was not humbled.

WRIGHT AND THE INTERNATIONAL STYLE

In 1932, Wright was invited to submit a design to what would become an epochal architectural exhibition at New York's Museum of Modern Art. It was organized by Philip Johnson and Henry-Russell Hitchcock and its title was 'The International Style', a name that was destined to stick.

The exhibition was intended to celebrate work by a new generation of mostly European architects, a group that included among others, Mies van der Rohe and Walter Gropius from Germany, J.J.P. Oud from Holland, and the French pair, Le Corbusier and Pierre Jeanneret.

The form of architecture they espoused, also widely known more simply as '**Modernism**', appeared in many ways to be diametrically opposed to Wright's. It celebrated industry and technology and had little time for craftsmanship. It saw itself as creating good, serious architecture for the masses. It celebrated the machine age and, in Le Corbusier's famous phrase, it saw the house as a machine for living in. It would be hard to imagine an ideology that Wright would have found more unsympathetic.

KEYWORD

Modernism: a late-nineteenth and twentieth century movement in all the arts, in which artists insisted on creating works that did not rely on previous historical models.

Wright's dismissal of the International Style was imperious and absolute. There is a famous story of him refusing to step foot in one of his own buildings because Gropius was there. More rationally, Wright criticized the architects of the International Style for creating soulless boxes, what he called 'cardboard architecture'. An equally telling criticism and one not only made by Wright, was that there was not actually anything very 'international' about this style at all. It was, in fact, narrowly European and theory-based, and Wright saw no reason why America should look to Europe for its ideas or its architecture. It offered itself as the universal solution to all architectural problems and Wright did not believe in universal solutions. There is something

Puritanical and humourless about the International Style that is never found in Wright's work.

Wright may also have had a more personal grudge against the Modernists. The emergence of these new European architectures inevitably suggested that he was no longer modern, no longer cutting edge and that his time had passed. Yet, the fact that he was invited to submit a design to the exhibition, suggests that even if he was no longer fashionable, he had certainly not been forgotten. Wright was definitely known to the architects of the International Style and generally admired by them. Even if the exhibition organizers felt lukewarm about his work, he remained a figure who could not be ignored.

There was much acrimony between Wright and the organizers. Ideology no doubt played a part, but another reason for the conflict may have been Wright's feeling that his work was not being given enough prominence. Nevertheless he did eventually submit a design, one that Philip Johnson thought was wonderful and well within the tenets of the International Style.

BROADACRE CITY

In the absence of real commissions, Wright turned his attention to some theoretical ones. He began to think in terms of large-scale social planning and he conceived a new kind of decentralized living: what he called Broadacre City.

In coming up with such a scheme, Wright may have been trying to show that he could compete with adherents of the International Style. Le Corbusier had devised the Ville Radieuse, another form of idealized urban planning consisting chiefly of geometrically arranged blocks of flats. Wright found these deeply unappealing.

Wright envisaged a model urban (or in reality suburban) environment, for a small, low-density population, yet large enough to support extensive arts and educational facilities. Each house, as the name suggests, was to be set on an acre (0.4 hectares) of land and the entire city would be just 10 km² (4 miles square). The problems of transporting people around this city would, in Wright's opinion, be easily solved by the motor car, although in a city of that size many journeys might be made on foot. An endless series of these modular cities could then be built end to end, as required, stitched together across the whole country, thereby avoiding what Wright saw as the horrors of large cities.

Today it is hard to see any particular brilliance in Wright's conception. Wright simply seems to be championing mass-suburbanization, a concept that large areas of the world now seem to have adopted, without any idealism and without any absolute benefits. For many, this process makes living in cities look increasingly appealing.

The one question that Wright's plan begged, and which has not been answered in practice, is how his urban modules would ever develop separate identities and why their inhabitants would think of themselves as members of separate 'communities' at all. The tendency for them to be essentially identical and interchangeable seems built into their conception.

Wright, in his time, had a slightly different problem with the scheme. There might be something profoundly democratic and American about each household having its own detached home and patch of land, but there was also thought to be something dangerously socialist about it. **Socialism** was certainly received more sympathetically in

> **KEYWORD**
>
> Socialism: a political theory advocating that land, property, capital and the means of production are owned jointly by the whole community.

America in the 1930s than it was later, but it was still viewed with suspicion and it was ever the province of cranks and utopians. Wright was happy to be seen as the latter but not the former.

One sometimes wonders to what extent Wright believed in Broadacre City as anything other than an exercise. Nevertheless, he built a model of such a city and it was widely exhibited, viewed with a kind of fascinated awe and the project engaged him intermittently for the rest of his life.

THE USONIAN HOUSE

A new, ideal kind of city would obviously require a new, ideal kind of house, and so Wright put his mind to designing what he called Usonian Houses. There is some speculation about where Wright got the name from, but it would seem to be a combination of United States of America (possibly of North America) and Utopia.

The Usonian Houses were a serious and, by and large, successful attempt to create low-cost housing, while adhering to Wright's architectural principles. They are modest houses, built with car ports rather than garages, for instance, but they are still impressive and they certainly do not look cheap or characterless. They were actually never as cheap as they might have been, since they were not mass produced and because Wright insisted on designing them individually and fitting each house to its site.

Even so there is much that the Usonian Houses have in common. Like the Prairie Houses, they tend to be long and low, without basements or attics, but the flat roofs and the expanses of glass are reminiscent of the International Style. They are single-storey, detached houses with a concrete slab for a foundation. Heating is supplied by a system of Wright's own invention that involves hot water pipes running through this concrete. They have a brick fireplace and brick piers at their core and then walls of batten and board are erected around them.

Typically, Usonian Houses are built on quite large plots of land and they turn inwards towards a central garden. Often they have floor to ceiling windows and large French doors. As ever, materials are allowed to speak for themselves, wood and stone remain unpainted.

The first Usonian House was built in 1936 for Herbert Jacobs, a journalist, and his wife Katherine. They approached Wright and asked if he could build a $5,500 house for 'ordinary people'. Of course,

Wright thought he could do anything and he agreed, and possibly he would have in any circumstances. However, the fact remained that he was not overburdened with other projects.

The Jacobs' House is a single-storey, flat roofed, L-shaped building which presents a flat, boldly featureless wall to the main road outside. It is not fortress-like in the manner of Hollyhock House, but it is a home that keeps itself to itself. The focus is on the garden in the arms of the L. The sense of roominess and light inside the house is spectacular and, again, there is that sense of not being sure of what is interior space and what is exterior.

Although Wright never got to build his Broadacre City, he was able to build a great many Usonian Houses (and a later version called the Usonian Automatic) in many locations throughout the United States. The last of them was built in the mid-1950s, by which time America was a very different country from the one in which Wright had first conceived their design. They are still lived in today and come on the market from time to time; some of them are sold at surprisingly affordable prices. Although the kind of people who live in them tend not to be completely 'ordinary' – they are usually serious fans of Wright and his architecture – they do not have to be millionaires either.

In fact the Jacobs were not such 'ordinary' people either. They wrote a book about the experience of having Wright build a house for them and they conducted public tours of their Usonian home, charging 50 cents a time. They calculated that this money soon paid for Wright's fee. This was something of a problem for Wright. The simple fact was that on a $5,500-house, an architect's commission would be very low and would not keep Wright in the style to which he had always been accustomed. Wright was happy to build modest houses, but was less happy to earn a modest income.

❋ ❋ ❋ SUMMARY ❋ ❋ ❋

- Wright married, then quickly divorced Miriam Noel. He met Olgivanna Hinzenberg, a woman with whom he would stay for the rest of his life.

- Wright had serious financial problems in the 1920s and 1930s, some of them created by Miriam Noel. Architectural commissions dried up.

- Wright lectured, wrote an autobiography and set up the Taliesin Foundation – an apprenticeship scheme for students of architecture.

- The emergence of the International Style of architecture left Wright even more beleaguered.

- Wright experimented with theoretical projects: Broadacre City and the Usonian House.

7 A Renaissance

Frank Lloyd Wright had always needed wealthy and indulgent patrons. At this desperate point in his career, a new one came along. Edgar Kaufmann Jr had briefly been one of the Taliesin apprentices. His stay was actually so short, it has been speculated that he was there to check out Wright on behalf of his father. Kaufmann Senior was a remarkable man, a Pittsburgh department store owner, a multimillionaire, a philanthropist and an enthusiastic supporter of interesting and risk-taking architects. He frequently employed architects to undertake civic projects, as well as houses and offices for himself. He was the kind of patron Wright was in great need of.

FALLINGWATER

In 1934, presumably having received a favourable report from his son, Kaufmann Senior approached Wright and suggested that they should work together on some public projects for Pittsburgh. These never came to fruition and, instead, Kaufmann asked Wright to build him a weekend cottage.

The Kaufmann family owned some land in Pennsylvania in a place called Bear Run, the main geographical feature being a spectacular waterfall. Kaufmann's idea, naturally enough, was that the cottage should have a view of these falls, but Wright had other ideas.

Wright visited the site a couple of times, but apparently had not started work on the final design when Edgar Kaufmann Sr called him at Taliesin on 22 September 1935. He said he was in Milwaukee, some 225 km (140 miles) miles away, and that he would like to drop in and see what progress had been made on his cottage.

In a reckless act, the stuff that legends are made of, Wright told Kaufmann that his house design was ready, despite not having a single

Fallingwater

thing on paper. In the amount of time it took Kaufmann to drive from Milwaukee to Spring Green, Wright sat down in the drafting studio, while his assistants looked on in wonder, and designed from scratch one of the most beautiful houses the world has ever seen: Fallingwater.

Wright's feat is remarkable enough, but it demonstrates that he designed buildings in his head rather than on paper. The plans and blueprints were simply a two-dimensional way of showing to others the things that already existed in his imagination. If Kaufmann was surprised by the design Wright offered him, he also had enough faith in Wright to accept it. He told Wright not to change a thing.

Wright had designed a house that scarcely offered a view of Kaufmann's waterfall at all. Instead, Fallingwater sits on top of the falls, straddles them with a series of cantilevered shelves that appear to float in space above the rocks and water, and are anchored by stone walls.

These 'shelves' offer a powerful horizontal emphasis in contrast to the vertical descent of the falls, and they are made of reinforced concrete, a material that was still regarded as new and untested at the time. However, when Kaufmann's engineers questioned the practicality of the design, Wright was offended and old Kaufmann that he did not deserve the house and threatened to terminate the project. Kaufmann submitted to Wright's genius. Time has shown that Kaufmann's engineers had got it just about right.

Nevertheless, what Kaufmann got for his money was a house that enabled him and his family to 'live intimately' with the falls, far more so than if the house simply offered a view of them. A suspended stairway leads directly from the living-room down to the stream. The floor of that room is of polished flagstones that imitate the look of water, and huge slabs of rock rise from it to become part of the hearth and fireplace.

One could argue that Fallingwater was inspired by the International Style and, if so, it was also an attempt to beat them at their own game. It contains certain Modernist touches; flat roofs, the use of reinforced concrete, cantilevers, (although Wright had previously used all of these features elsewhere) and it does have a somewhat machine-made look. Yet, it also seems to be a part of nature, inspired by the site, coming out of the rock and still floating in space. It is the perfect expression of Wright's organic architecture, the perfect balance between the natural and the built environment.

From its very inception the house created enormous publicity for Wright, almost all of it favourable, and it was well enough received to find its way on to the cover of *Time* magazine. It does seem odd that in the middle of an economic depression, America would take to its heart a millionaire's holiday cottage. One can only assume that Fallingwater was so undeniably beautiful that it disarmed criticism based on envy. Perhaps it was also a reminder to Americans that, even in the middle of a depression, theirs was still a country in which great things were possible.

Wright was suddenly celebrated as a great American architect. An article about Fallingwater in the St Louis Dispatch of 1937 called him 'the venerable dean of Modernism'. America was apparently ready to forgive him those earlier scandals and indiscretions; he was after all nearly 70 years old. But a distinguished retirement was not Wright's style. He still had over 20 productive years ahead of him, years in which he would create some of his finest work.

THE JOHNSON WAX BUILDING

If Fallingwater was a rich man's indulgence, then another project Wright worked on at this time was more like a worker's paradise. The Administration Building that he created for the Johnson Wax Company in Racine, Wisconsin in 1936 was the largest project he had been involved with for some years.

The Johnson company had the reputation of a progressive, benevolent employer and Wright seemed to be the ideal architect for the project, but he had to fight off another architect before he got the commission. Indeed, Wright's first idea was to abandon the site that the company actually owned in order to build a workers' city instead, something along the lines of his Broadacre scheme. Wiser, or at least less ambitious, counsel prevailed, although this was still one of the projects where Wright went wildly over budget.

Since the building was to be sited in an unattractive industrial setting, Wright, as with the much earlier Larkin Building in Buffalo, created a self-contained, inward-looking structure. The Johnson Administration Building presents a closed, inscrutable face to the world. Whereas Fallingwater and the Usonian houses are all straight lines and right angles, this was to be a sleek, streamlined building, that does indeed have a waxed, polished finish to it.

The walls are of red brick and there are no windows as such, but just below roof level are bands of horizontally arranged Pyrex glass tubes that let light in without offering a view out. These were an innovation

The Johnson Wax Building

and created considerable problems. Strips of sealant originally ran between each tube, but these were notorious for leaking, and this may have been the cause of Wright's widespread reputation for making buildings that let in water. The sealant was eventually replaced with rubber gaskets that solved the problem.

What makes the building so spectacular, however, is less the outside than the single large central space within; a 'great workroom' as Wright called it, over 36 by 60 metres (120 by 200 feet). As so often with Wright, this is approached through a modest, low-ceilinged entrance hall that gives little indication of the wonders to come. Some say this workroom looks like a cathedral. Others describe it as like being a woodland glade or an aquarium. It is a huge, magical room bathed in soft, transcendent light.

From ground level one looks up into a forest of tall, concrete columns that are variously described as looking like lily pads or mushrooms. These really are extraordinary structures; elegant, futuristic, totally unfamiliar. Set on a grid throughout the space, 6m (20 feet) apart, they measure just 23 cm (9 inches) in diameter at the base. They rise up, broadening slightly as they ascend, and finally they flatten out into a huge cap that is 5.6 m (18.5 feet) across. These caps are then connected to each other by beams that span the 46 cm (18 inch) gaps between them. Light then floods down through these gaps from the skylight overhead.

Wright's reputation as an engineer rests on these strange, yet sturdy, columns. It is said that he did not do any mathematical calculations when designing them. He somehow simply knew they would do the job. In fact they would never have to support a very great deal of weight. There are no floors above the workroom, so each column was simply required to support a 1.85 m^2 (20 foot square) section of roof, along with however much snow the Wisconsin winter deposited on it.

Nevertheless, the Wisconsin building authorities were unconvinced by these columns and so Wright cast one column and held a demonstration of its strength. It was a very public demonstration, attended by members of the building and architectural industry, along with members of the national press and the public. Wright was in his element.

The column was erected and sandbags were hoisted up and placed around the edge of the cap. The building inspectors required it to take a weight of 12,200 kg (12 tons), which it very soon did, but Wright was not satisfied with that. He had an audience and he wanted to put on a show.

Sandbags weighing 30,500 kg (30 tons) were placed on top of the column, then loose sand, then lumps of pig iron. Wright then walked over to the column, kicked it and hit it with his cane. His confidence was well justified. By the end of the demonstration a weight of 70,000 kg (60 tons) had been loaded on the column, and it collapsed only after the removal of one of the wooden, non-load bearing braces that held it in position.

It was a total vindication for Wright's skill as an engineer, but this explains very little about the success of that space, one that the architect, Philip Johnson, describes as the finest room in America. Its startling beauty and elegance is not simply a matter of concrete and stresses. It demonstrates that architecture is about something far more important and yet also less tangible than that.

The Johnson Administration Building was a great attention-grabbing building, both for the architect and the client. It was another very public success for Wright. The building was featured in *Life* magazine who described it as 'Spectacular as the showiest Hollywood set'.

WRIGHT GOES WEST AGAIN

Wright's creativity and energy remained undiminished, but by the late 1930s his health was starting to falter. He found the Wisconsin winters difficult to cope with and he was looking for a way to spend some time in a warmer climate, specifically Arizona.

He already knew parts of that desert state because of the work he had done on the Arizona Biltmore hotel and the San Marcos-in-the-Desert project. While engaged on the latter, Wright and his apprentices had set up a desert camp, a tent city which they called Ocatillo. Creating shelter from scratch in the desert was no doubt an immensely educational challenge for the apprentices, but now Wright began to imagine a more permanent desert base.

Wright's attraction to the desert needs no great amount of explanation. It was a new world, a new frontier, a place that was elemental and untouched, a blank sheet on which he could make his mark. Those, like Wright, who were suspicious of the joys of the city, would inevitably find the desert a welcome revelation. At the same time, building in the desert would clearly be no easy matter. That Wright should want to take on these difficulties and this harsh environment when he was over 70 was not merely brave and optimistic, it was positively heroic.

TALIESIN WEST

In 1937 he bought 325 hectares (800 acres) of desert outside Scottsdale in Arizona, close to Phoenix in the southern foothills of the McDowell mountain range. It was a place that he said, 'offered a view over the rim of the world'. The land cost $3.50 per acre, a bargain price even then, because no water had ever been found on the property. But Wright employed a well-digger and after an expensive search, water was duly found. From 1938 onwards, there was an annual migration of Wright and his apprentices, a somewhat ramshackle motor caravan that moved from Taliesin in Wisconsin to what was to become known as Taliesin West.

As with the original Taliesin, this work was in constant progress. There was never a blueprint or grand design, at least not outside of Wright's head. He improvised designs as he went along, sometimes sketching plans in the evening and getting the apprentices to put them into action the next day.

The stretch of desert that Wright bought was certainly long and low, but it had nothing in common with his native Midwest. Wright spoke in his autobiography of the 'dotted line' of the desert, and this is a strikingly brilliant observation and a great piece of description. There is a continuous roughness and jaggedness to the desert that Wright's architecture at Taliesin West imitates and celebrates.

These days, the first sighting of Taliesin West can be strangely disappointing. You might have imagined 'great architecture', something that stood out from the desert and drew attention to itself. In fact it is a muted and, in some ways, an inconspicuous structure, not one building but many that straggle asymmetrically across the desert. Their shapes and colours are those of the landscape, and there is something camouflaged about it.

Largely this is because of the materials Wright used, chiefly what has come to be known as desert concrete or desert rubblestone. Large rocks were taken from the desert floor and then placed inside wooden forms into which concrete was poured. When the concrete was set and the wood was removed, a wall was left in which the rock faces were revealed. Since the rocks had been picked up from the surrounding desert, the building was quite literally part of the landscape, and the landscape part of the building.

Taliesin West, Wright's summer home and studio, Pheonix, Arizona

This was not merely decorative, but a solution to a substantial problem. Wright needed building materials and few were easily available. Desert rock was plentiful, but it was difficult to cut or shape and such a task was, in any case, beyond the skills of the apprentices. However, many of the rocks did have one flat surface and this could be used to form the outer face of the wall, while the curved surface of the other side was turned to the centre. These walls are in fact exquisitely beautiful and, although they look perfectly natural, Wright was not above using acid to bring out the colour of some of the rocks. Where he needed structures that could not be built from rock, he used redwood beams, which appear throughout Taliesin West, looking like a series of angular spines.

The apprentices had a massive job on their hands building Taliesin West, but they took to it with characteristic enthusiasm. They built 275 m (900 feet) of desert concrete wall. They laid roads. Rocks containing **petroglyphs** were

KEYWORD

Petroglyphs: rock carvings.

found on the land and these were transported back to base; a particularly fine one stands by the entrance gate. When cacti stood in the way of their progress, these had to be relocated and transplanted, and some of them were massive.

Eventually, Wright and his apprentices spent about half the year at Taliesin West, and each annual visit brought new ideas and new revisions. In Wright's original conception, every room was to be open to the desert, completely blurring distinctions between inside and outside. Various canvas awnings and blinds were slid in and out of place as required. If this sounds unnecessarily makeshift, it has to be remembered that Wright used the place only in winter, a season when the heat would be relatively mild. He also intended at first that there should be no glass anywhere in the structure, but by 1945 he was becoming a bit less dogmatic about this and glass replaced some of the canvas. Today, the building is used all year-round and there is plenty of glass and plastic, and even air-conditioning.

Taliesin West is a complex of buildings linked by open terraces and wide walkways, with pools and a sunken garden. As well as the substantial Wright family living quarters, there is a drafting room, an office, an apprentices' compound, a machine shop, dark rooms and a laundry unit. There is a music pavilion with seating for 100 people, a small and exquisite 'cabaret theatre' half sunk into the ground. Since the building is still in use by the Taliesin Foundation and not merely kept as a shrine, many of these structures have been changed since Wright's time, but Wright would surely have approved of that, not least because it shows that Taliesin West continues to thrive as a practical working building.

The garden room was, and remains, the highlight. It is 17.5 m (56 feet) long, and varies in width from 10.5 m (35 feet) to 7.5 m (25 feet). Early photographs show it to have been entirely open to the elements, without walls or ceiling, with shelter provided by canvas flaps that were operated by ropes. There was always a large fireplace (naturally), and a grand piano. Today there is a translucent roof, and the room looks considerably less rugged than the one Wright imagined, but it is still a stunning interior that opens out to the desert beyond.

Today, the suburban sprawl of Scottsdale has edged right up to the boundary of the Taliesin West estate. In some ways the houses of Scottsdale might have been at home in a version of Broadacre City – individual houses on large lots, but there is little that is Usonian about them. They tend to be stucco-clad, ranch-style houses, often with a **Spanish mission** or **adobe** influence. Wright would have been appalled. But it is still possible to see that, in its original state, Taliesin West must have been a truly magical and **quixotic** place; a complicated, gorgeously improbable oasis in the middle of absolutely nowhere.

Taliesin West is, in many ways, Wright's most characteristic and idiosyncratic work. It is not as grand as his most famous work and it was not conceived with the same personal passion that he brought to the original Taliesin, yet it is a creation that embodies the great intensity of the Wright spirit.

KEYWORDS

Spanish mission: architectural style of the missions established by Spanish Franciscans in Florida, Texas, Arizona, New Mexico and California in the late-eighteenth and early-nineteenth centuries. Facades could be ornate, but the general effect was of simplicity.

Adobe: literally an unburned brick dried in the sun. As a style of architecture it refers to the mud-walled structures of the American southwest and Mexico.

Quixotic: literally in the manner of Don Quixote. Figuratively, striving for lofty and visionary ideals.

❊ ❊ ❊ SUMMARY ❊ ❊ ❊

● Wright found a patron in Edgar Kaufmann Sr and built Fallingwater for him.

● Fallingwater is one of the most beautiful houses in the world, an embodiment of all of Wright's architectural principles.

● Wright began to spend time in the Arizona desert, buying land and creating Taliesin West, a winter base that he and his apprentices built using materials from the desert itself.

The Long Final Flourish

8

As the 1930s ended, Wright was more in demand as an architect than he had been for years. In 1939 and 1940 he completed 19 commissions in places as diverse as Arizona, California, Missouri and New Jersey. Some of these were comparatively modest, indeed some of them were Usonian houses, but others were far more substantial. Auldbrass Plantation, for example, built in Yemassee, South Carolina was a large estate with stables, kennels and an aviary, as well as elaborate living quarters that made use of native cypress for the walls and copper tiles on the roof.

Even the Second World War slowed Wright down only temporarily. He hated the war, of course. He was a pacifist, but more than that, he was an isolationist. He was not merely against war, he was also against what he saw as the corrupt motives of the British Empire. He made some sweeping and ill-advised public statements and there was even an article written for the British press which came close to suggesting that the German bombing of London was just what that city deserved.

By 1941, however, it did not much matter what Wright thought. All able-bodied young men had to register for the draft, and this included 26 of the Taliesin apprentices. This affected Wright far more profoundly than the destruction of European cities. He tried to

KEYWORD

Seditious: from sedition, a concerted effort to overthrow a government.

have his apprentices exempted on the grounds that they were needed for farm work, but his request was turned down. Several apprentices who shared Wright's pacifist views ended up in jail for draft evasion, although others duly joined the war effort. Wright, meanwhile, came under scrutiny from the FBI for his potentially **seditious** influence on young Americans.

Nevertheless, some buildings were completed during the war years. In 1938 Wright had begun work on the Florida Southern College in Lakeland, Florida, and parts of the campus continued to be built throughout the war. There was another house for the Jacobs family, the couple who had commissioned the first Usonian House. And in 1944, Wright built a Research Tower for the Johnson Wax Company to accompany the highly regarded Administration Building. This new Johnson commission proved to be as remarkable a building in its way as the previous one, a high-rise cantilevered structure, with 14 levels; seven of them solid square floors and seven of them circular mezzanines like balconies above the squares. Its outside has the same smooth, streamlined look as the Administration Building, but claims can be made for its organic nature. Some say it is like a tree, with a central trunk containing stairs, an elevator and services, while the floors extend like branches.

After 1945, America enjoyed an unprecedented economic boom, a great deal of new architecture was built and Wright was able to take full advantage. The next 15 years were by far the busiest and most productive of his life. In that time he designed a scarcely believable 350 buildings, saying he could just 'shake them out of his sleeve'.

Some of these designs were simply fanciful, for instance a scheme for a 1.6 km (1 mile) high skyscraper in Chicago, which would apparently have required razing much of the city to provide a car park. Nonetheless, some rather fanciful designs did indeed get built, such as the Civic Center in Marin County, California – the only building Wright ever built for the US government. It is an amazing futuristic complex with a domed library, a circular post office and a tall pre-Colombian style pylon that was also a radio antenna. There was also the very eccentric Price Company Tower in Bartlesville, Oklahoma; a 19-storey high-rise based on a 1929 design intended for New York, known as St Mark's-in-the-Bouwerie.

There were a number of religious buildings in this period: a Greek Orthodox church in Wauwatosa, Wisconsin; the Beth Sholom Synagogue in Elkins Park, Pennsylvania and the Minor Chapel at the Florida Southern College. And always there were private residences: the Meyer residence in Michigan, shaped like a drum and the Davis Residence in Indiana, based on the design of an Indian teepee, among many others. There were also what Wright referred to as his 'Usonian Automatic' houses.

Wright was still trying to come up with a means of mass producing elegant affordable architecture. The basis of the Usonian Automatic was a hollow block system, a familiar enough idea for Wright, but these were to be lighter than anything he had used before. The intention was that they should be simple enough to allow construction by a self-builder. However, in the event, these blocks were not at all simple to use and required skills that were likely to be far beyond the capabilities of any self-builder. The most successful of the Usonian Automatics is probably the Benjamin Adelman House, built in Phoenix in 1951, which looks like a stripped down version of Wright's Los Angeles textile block houses. Yet this hardly qualifies as cheap mass-produced housing; Wright was aiming for a house that cost $5000, the Adelman House cost $25,000.

Wright was not alone in trying to create affordable housing. In post-war America, many agreed with Wright that the cities were terrible places and a lot of people were moving to the suburbs. The Federal Housing Association and the Veterans' Administration were making it easy for returning GIs to buy their own homes, and the demand for housing was enormous. In such a market there was much room for shoddy or downright unscrupulous developers and architects. Wright was sincere in his desire to operate in that sphere, but he was constitutionally incapable of producing anything cheap or shoddy.

FAME AND RECOGNITION

Wright had become a star architect, a grand old man, a living (and working) national treasure. There was constant travel, including a trip to Baghdad to discuss the building of an opera house there and a visit to Wales where he received an honorary degree from the University of Wales. This was one of many. Yale, Princeton, Cooper Union and Florida Southern College were just some of the others. Wright was endlessly being given awards, medals and other honours, and in 1956 Richard Daley, the mayor of Chicago, declared 17 October to be Frank Lloyd Wright Day.

In a wildly uncharacteristic acceptance speech to the American Institute of Architects in 1948, Wright said, 'As these honours have descended upon me one by one, somehow I expected each honour would add a certain lustre, a certain brightness to the psyche which is mine. On the contrary a shadow seems to fall with each one. I think it casts a shadow on my native arrogance, and for a moment I feel coming on that disease which is recommended so highly, of humility ...' (*Journal of the American Instituite of Architects*, Vol XI, No. 5, May 1949, pp. 199–207). Perhaps he could at last afford to be humble.

Wright's relationship with Olgivanna remained utterly sound, if occasionally turbulent. Wright relied on his wife for the smooth running of both his life and his two homes, set over 1600 km (1,000 miles) apart. However, neither was an easygoing character. There were occasional outbursts of jealousy, sometimes sexual and sometimes for other reasons.

When Olgivanna published a book in 1955 called *The Struggle Within* (Horizon), Wright was childishly angry. He was sneering and contemptuous and said that she ought to be content with just being his wife. Olgivanna was enough of a feminist that she threatened to leave him over this. No doubt Wright felt threatened. He was almost 90 years old, his wife was much younger. He may have resented her for becoming a public figure in her own right and stealing his limelight –

a slightly absurd notion given the extent of his fame and achievement – but a greater resentment was surely that she had far more years ahead of her than he did. Perhaps he was simply experiencing intimations of mortality.

Wright remained a great self-publicist. He continued to write and lecture, and he published a stream of books, including *The Future of Architecture* (1953), *The Natural House* (1954) and *The Living City* (1958). He also began to appear on television. In the recordings that survive, Wright seems an immensely natural and charismatic performer. He certainly looks much more relaxed and at home in the new medium, than do the people interviewing him. He seems to twinkle and he smiles a lot. He seems grand and he is certainly not modest, but there is something impish about him as well. One certainly does not see the 'embarrassing Portrait of the Artist as a Joke' that Peter Blake described (see Chapter 1).

THE GUGGENHEIM

Perhaps Wright's much proclaimed hatred of cities should not be taken entirely at face value. It is hard to imagine that anyone who really cared about architecture could find New York City uninspiring. Wright was also enough of a realist to know that, in order to absolutely secure his reputation as a world class architect, he needed to have a major building in New York. The opportunity came with the Guggenheim Museum, a work first commissioned in 1943 but not completed until after Wright's death.

Solomon R. Guggenheim, who had made a fortune in his family mining and import business, had retired from commerce and amassed a large international collection of 'non-objective' works of art by the likes of Vasily Kandinsky, Max Ernst and Hans Richter. He wanted it displayed in a suitably impressive building. A woman called Hilla Rebay was curator of the collection and the prime mover behind creating a museum.

Rebay thought that Wright was the ideal architect for the project and that he would bring the appropriate high-minded spiritual qualities to the job. She, Wright and Guggenheim were in general agreement about the principles of the museum, but progress was slow. Guggenheim was understandably reluctant to commit himself to a major project while the war was continuing, but even after it ended he was hesitant to start work. By 1949 things had begun to move a little, but then Guggenheim died and the project was left in limbo. Solomon's nephew, Harry G. Guggenheim, was appointed president of the museum's foundation and there was some slight progress. However, at this point Hilla Rebay fell out with Wright and was replaced as future director of the museum with James Johnson Sweeney taking her place.

Whereas Rebay, at least initially, had been a supporter of Wright's design, Sweeney was concerned with what he saw as its shortcomings. Wright's design went through considerable changes, however, quite early on he chose a helical structure, wider at the top than the bottom, although an early drawing shows it narrowing rather than widening. The Guggenheim is often said to resemble a snail or a seashell, but it looks equally like a drum or a cooking pot. Internally there is a great central cavity, lit by a huge skylight. Around the edges of the space is a continuous circular ramp, rising steadily to the top.

Wright's original intention was that visitors should take the lift to the top floor and then walk down the ramp through the exhibition. Contemporary exhibitions almost never use the building this way. The Guggenheim is a very popular museum and the lifts are small. Exhibitions tend to be arranged chronologically or sequentially from the bottom to the top. This can sometimes lead to a sense of anticlimax. Once at the top, there is nothing to do but come down again. On the other hand one does walk through the exhibition twice and it is always fascinating to see how your perspective on the way down is different from how it was on the way up.

Sweeney was simply concerned that the Guggenheim might not be a very good space in which to view art. The continually rising (or falling) ramp means that the viewer is generally standing on a sloping floor while looking at the paintings. The walls of the gallery slope outwards and so paintings either have to be suspended some way out from the wall, or they are mounted flush and they slope backwards. Wright at one point claimed that this was his intention all along, that he had devised a new way of looking at paintings, but one has to wonder if he really believed that.

A group of contemporary artists protested about the design, saying they did not want their work displayed in such a place. They feared that the building would overwhelm their art, while Wright said that the building would inspire them to do better work. Both sides had an excellent point.

Wright was not a fan of modern art, indeed apart from Japanese prints he was against putting art on the walls of his buildings. He was not entirely sympathetic to the aims of the museum and it shows. The Guggenheim is undoubtedly a difficult environment in which to show art. The imposing nature of Wright's creation can be a distraction. It is certainly a building in which minor or second-rate art can look utterly lost. But then, why would Wright have created a building that flattered minor or second-rate art?

Artists were not the only ones with objections. Other, greater, problems were caused by the New York building authorities. Much like the men responsible for supervizing the Johnson Wax Administration Building, they had never seen anything like the design for the Guggenheim, but then who had? They obviously had no experience of supervizing the construction of such a building and so they fretted about many things, including the strength of the concrete, the sloping ramps, and the way the building would project 1.5 m (5 feet) further into the street at the top than at the bottom.

Negotiations dragged on and might have reached stalemate if Robert Moses had not stepped in. He was New York's construction co-ordinator, with certain family connections to Wright and, according to legend, he cleared the deadlock by saying, 'Damn it, get a permit for Frank. I don't care how many laws you have to break. I want the Guggenheim built'. And it was.

The Guggenheim is, in many ways, an outrageous building, a low curved structure in a city of tall vertical lines. It is a playful piece of architecture in a city that is all business. A loud attention-grabbing building that makes all the others around it serve as a mere backdrop; quite a feat in itself. Yet for all of its originality, it contains many features familiar from Wright's earlier work; a building that was essentially windowless, a central open space surrounded by ranked balconies with light flooding in from above. And, above all, the Guggenheim shows Wright's genius for using concrete, demonstrating what a plastic, sculptural and flexible medium it can be.

Ground was finally broken on the Guggenheim site in 1956, but Wright did not live to see it completed. Frank Lloyd Wright died quite suddenly in April 1959, after a minor operation to remove an intestinal blockage. However, perhaps no operation is minor for a man of 91 and, although there were no complications and no apparent danger, Wright died a couple of days later. In fact, those close to him had been concerned about his health for some time. He had been suffering from Meniere's syndrome with its accompanying dizziness, nausea and the loss of balance. His end, however, was perfectly decorous. According to the night nurse on duty at the hospital, 'He just sighed – and died.' Olgivanna threw herself into the task of preserving and burnishing Wright's reputation, a task that she continued up until her own death.

It may seem extraordinary to say that a man of Wright's age died at the height of his powers, but as far as creating architecture was concerned, things had seldom been better for him. His reputation could scarcely have been greater, his work was much sought after, he was engaged in

The Guggenheim, New York

numerous projects and he had unbuilt designs on hand, some of which are still available today.

As recently as 1996, for example, a passive solar house was built in Hawaii, following plans that Wright had originated in 1954. The Frank Lloyd Wright Foundation certified it as an original Frank Lloyd Wright design and guaranteed that it would not be duplicated. His legacy does not simply live on, it continues to thrive and renew itself.

---

* * *SUMMARY * * *

- After the Second World War Wright took full advantage of the building boom in America.

- In the last 15 years of his life, Wright designed 350 buildings.

- Wright became the grand old man of American Architecture.

- The Guggenheim Museum was a great final monument, Wright's only substantial work in New York City.

Frank Lloyd Wright and Organic Architecture

9

Frank Lloyd Wright was a champion of, a proselytizer for, and arguably the inventor of what he called 'organic architecture', although the term does also appear in the works of John Ruskin. The term is so immediately appealing to a modern audience concerned with conservation and worried about preserving the environment and its scarce resources, that there is a tendency to read our own contemporary ideas into what Wright might have meant. We want to believe that to be organic is to be natural, to be 'environmentally friendly'. Although this is certainly part of Wright's credo, it is by no means the whole story.

Wright's concept of 'organic architecture' was a work in progress, much like his home Taliesin, a developing set of working practices and philosophical opinions, rather than a rigid dogma. He wrote about it constantly throughout his career and there are times when he seems merely to use organic as a synonym for 'good'. At other times, he seems to mean simply architecture by Frank Lloyd Wright.

However, a serviceable definition comes from a piece that Wright published quite early in his career in *Architectural Record* in March 1908. He wrote, 'I still believe that the ideal of an organic architecture forms the origin and source, the strength and, fundamentally, the significance of everything ever worthy the name of architecture.

'By organic architecture I mean an architecture that *develops* from within outward in harmony with the conditions of its being as distinguished from one that is *applied* from without.'

Put another way, Wright believed that a building was a solution to a set of problems. These problems arose out of the nature of the site, the purpose of the building, the availability of materials and resources and so on. The solution was to be intrinsic, pragmatic, and found in situ, not something imposed by an architect in accordance with some pre-existing, external theory. As Wright told Edgar Tafel, 'What we did yesterday we won't do today. And what we don't do tomorrow will not be what we'll be doing the day after.' (Reported in Tafel's book *Apprentice to Genius*, McGraw-Hill, New York, 1979.)

In some ways this sounds so utterly reasonable that there is a tendency to think that Wright is merely stating the obvious, that architecture must be a practical art, that buildings should suit their location and should be matched to their function. How else, you might ask, should buildings be designed? What else should an architect do? Yet Wright's stance was, and remains, far less common than one would like to believe.

As we have seen, this was one of Wright's chief objections to the so-called International Style. It imposed a single, limited solution on a multitude of different problems. Its practitioners had devised one form of building and they were arrogant enough to believe that these were buildings for all seasons. Wright would have none of that.

Contemporary architects are scarcely immune to this one-size-fits-all approach. Frank Gehry, to take an obvious example, evidently thinks that undulating titanium walls are just the thing, whether on the outside of an art museum (as in the Guggenheim in Bilbao) or in the inside of a cafeteria (in the Condé Nast Building in New York).

For Wright, the choice of site was all important. 'Then standing on that site,' he wrote, 'look about you so that you see what has charm. What is the reason to build there? Find out. Then build your house so that you may still look from where you stood upon all that charmed you and lose nothing of what you saw before the house was built but see more. Architectural associations accentuate the character of the landscape if the architecture is right.' (Quoted in *Taliesin West: In the Realm of Ideas*, Frank Lloyd Wright Foundation, 1993.) Who could argue with that?

Wright's Prairie Houses emphasized the connection between the building and the landscape. The Midwest is long, low and flat, and so it was appropriate that the buildings Wright made there should share these attributes. His best buildings do not so much sit on the earth, but emerge from it, grow out of it. Sometimes it is hard to see where the building ends and the landscape starts.

The most extreme and successful example of this is surely Taliesin West, with its walls made of desert concrete, incorporating rocks picked up from the desert. This was part of Wright's laudable intention of letting materials speak for themselves, let them be what they are. He rejected disguise or pretense. Wood was waxed, but not painted. Stone walls were left exposed with rough edges. Even though he performs unexpected miracles with concrete, you never forget that it is indeed concrete. It is never concrete pretending to be something else.

And if Wright is always concerned with bringing the natural into his architecture, there are many times when he introduces the positively elemental. Earth and air are perhaps a given in any work of architecture, but Wright's buildings seem simultaneously earthier and airier than most. Water is frequently added in the form of pools and ponds; a waterfall at Fallingwater, a diverted canal at Auldbrass Plantation and a water feature in the hearth at Hollyhock House. And then, very often, there is fire too. It is probable that no domestic house by Wright does not have a substantial fireplace at its heart. They even cropped up in the more public buildings, such as the Imperial Hotel in Tokyo.

There are, however, some fairly obvious objections to Wright's definition of organic and some contradictions in the buildings he actually designed. One feels that he sometimes talked a much better game than he played, and this was probably inherent in his personality. Although he wished to blend in with nature, he also wanted to stand out from it. He was a peacock, not a chameleon. And this sometimes applied to his buildings too.

One can always argue that architecture is an inherently unnatural form. It is, by definition, an imposition on nature. Many natural landscapes, we might say, would be far better off if they did not have pieces of architecture in them.

Fallingwater, for instance, is a magnificent creation, it certainly looks at home in its environment and by any reckoning it is one of the world's most startling houses. Nevertheless, it is set in the centre of thousands of acres of previously untouched forest. It is easy to make the case that the environment would have been better served by remaining untouched.

Perhaps the simple and obvious defence to this, is that humans are part of nature, they will inevitably live and build on the land and so it would be best if they lived and built harmoniously, as Wright claimed his architecture would allow people to do. If he had not created Fallingwater, then another architect would have created something far less sympathetic. Of course, when Wright talked about architecture being natural, he was not suggesting that we live in caves. The architect's purpose, as he saw it, was to create a building that contained the same spirit, harmony and order found in nature.

However, in the particular case of Fallingwater, which was intended to co-exist harmoniously with a waterfall, Wright's idea of co-existence was to build the house actually on top of the falls. You can not see the waterfall without also seeing his house. From the house itself it is hard to see the waterfall at all. House and waterfall look stunning when seen together, yet one feels that the falls are there to beautify the house rather than vice versa.

Wright was certainly willing to entertain projects that were anything but environmentally friendly. One of these was a monstrous project known as the Gordon Strong Automobile Objective. Gordon Strong, a wealthy Chicago businessman, owned a piece of land that included a peak known as Sugar Loaf Mountain. He asked Wright to design a building to go on top of this mountain, something that would 'serve as an objective for short motor trips'.

The design went through many stages before being abandoned as impractical and too expensive. Essentially Wright planned to build a cantilevered road that spiralled up to the peak of the mountain, where it was variously thought there might be a dance hall, theatre or planetarium. The final destination did not much matter, however. It was the getting there that counted.

Wright envisaged 'people sitting comfortably in their own cars in a novel circumstance with the whole landscape revolving about them, as exposed to view as though they were in an aeroplane.' (Letter from Frank Lloyd Wright to Gordon Strong, 20 October 1925, filed with Strong's papers, Stronghold Inc, Dickerson, Maryland.)

One can imagine that the view from the roadway would be spectacular, if a little distracting for the driver, as he negotiated the tight curves. Nonetheless would not have destroyed everybody else's view of the mountain? Wright may not have thought so. He might have argued that nature with one of his structures in it, was nature improved, but it is probable that even he would have lost that particular argument.

The spiral or helical form emerged again in the Guggenheim Museum, another building that has an uneasy relationship with its environment. It can certainly be argued that the shape is organic in so far as it derives from nature, but in what conceivable sense is the finished building in harmony with the environment of urban Manhattan? It is a low-rise, curvilinear building in a city that is all square blocks and towering verticals. In that sense, Mies van der Rohe's Seagram Tower, a building that Wright would have affected to despise, is far more at home in its setting.

The truth is, the Guggenheim was built to stand out, not to blend in at all. It was meant to draw attention to itself and to Wright's prowess as an architect. And it does. The surrounding architecture of New York is only there to provide contrast, to make Wright's building look even more startling. This is not so terrible. The ploy works magnificently and the effect is undoubtedly dazzling, but the building remains anomalous, a brilliant curiosity. There is no building like it in New York (indeed there are no buildings like it anywhere else either) and Wright rejoiced in that fact, as do many users and admirers of the building, but we should be very wary of calling it organic.

The textile block houses that Wright built in Los Angeles in the 1920s seem to be a special case again. It is hard to say exactly what would constitute 'organic' in Los Angeles. It seems the least 'natural' of cities. Wright's houses stand out there just as much as the Guggenheim does in New York. They exist as examples of thrilling exoticism, gloriously strange and substantial pieces of architecture in an environment that is all too often bland and transient.

When it came to the creation of his own homes at Taliesin and Taliesin West, the definition of organic seems to take on a rather specialized meaning. The buildings do blend harmoniously with the landscapes, but in both cases Wright acquired hundreds of acres of land and made them his own. At Taliesin, in particular, he was able to look out from the buildings he had created and know that he owned and controlled everything he saw.

Two much-told anecdotes go some way towards demonstrating Wright's attitude. The first concerns the Guernsey cows on the estate at Taliesin which were not producing enough milk. The farm manager suggested that they introduce some Holstein cattle which would improve the yield. Wright was outraged. Holstein cattle are black and white and, in his opinion, they would ruin the look of the landscape. Black and white did not look good against green. Only Guernseys, being brown and cream, would produce the correct visual effect.

The other story concerns Wright's broadcasting of music around the landscape of Taliesin. While he worked in his drafting room, he constantly played the music of Bach and Beethoven, and one day he decided that the field workers should share this pleasure too. He set up a loudspeaker on top of the Romeo and Juliet windmill, which he had built as a young man, and filled the surrounding countryside with music, whether anyone wanted it or not.

Wright's sister, Jane Porter, who lived nearest to the windmill, complained bitterly about this imposition, and did eventually get her way, but only after a struggle. Wright simply could not believe that anyone did not share his tastes and, if they disagreed with him in matters of music or anything else, they were obviously wrong.

These two stories are less trivial than they might at first seem. They demonstrate Wright's desire to control absolutely everything in his environment. This may have been part of the reason for his professed hatred of cities; there were just too many things in the urban environment that were impossible to control.

While there is nothing inherently wrong in choosing farm animals for their aesthetic appeal or with imposing music on a landscape, neither suggests an easygoing relationship with the environment. Given the opportunity, Wright dominated nature rather than became part of it.

He was, perhaps, like one of the great eighteenth-century English landscape gardeners, a **Capability Brown**, although of course in Wright's case he had built the great house to which the landscape was attached. Like Brown, Wright viewed the natural environment as a source of inspiration and his work was, therefore, nature perfected. Clearly by 'organic' Wright also meant intuitive and he believed that his intuition was better than anybody else's.

KEYWORDS

Capability Brown: the best known British eighteenth-century naturalistic landscape gardener whose work is seen at Stowe and Blenheim Palace. The nickname came from his habit of saying that places had 'capabilities'.

Let us give Frank Lloyd Wright the last word, in this passage from *An Organic Architecture*, published in 1939, 'What is architecture anyway? Is it the vast collection of the various buildings which have been built to please the varying taste of the various lords of mankind? I think not.

No, I know that architecture is life; or at least it is life itself taking form and therefore it is the truest record of life as it was lived in the world yesterday, as it is lived today or ever will be lived. So architecture I know to be a Great Spirit.'

* * * SUMMARY * * *

● Wright spoke of 'organic architecture' throughout his life, but it was a developing set of ideas rather than a dogmatic theory.

● Essentially 'organic architecture' involves an architecture that is harmonious within its parts and with its environment. It displays a sense of order that Wright found in nature.

● Sometimes Wright's own buildings are not quite as harmonious or organic as he would have had us believe.

GLOSSARY

Adobe Literally an unburned brick dried in the sun. As a style of architecture it refers to the mud-walled structures of the American southwest and Mexico.

Arts and Craft movement Initially a London-based movement centred on the Arts and Crafts Exhibition Society. It reacted against the dehumanizing effects of late-nineteenth century industrialization, insisting on craftsmanship and truth to materials.

Avant-garde Literally the vanguard of an army, figuratively the latest wave of experimentation in an art form.

Butt-glazed Corner windows that abut each other without a mullion; part of Wright's desire to destroy the box-like nature of rooms.

Capability Brown The best known British eighteenth-century naturalistic landscape gardener whose work is seen at Stowe and Blenheim Palace. The nickname came from his habit of saying that places had 'capabilities'.

Clerestory A row of windows, originally found in churches – between the top of a structure's wall and its roof – to allow light into a tall, otherwise poorly illuminated space.

Froebel kindergarten Froebel was a German educator and founder of the kindergarten. He believed in 'self-activity' and play as essential for children's education, the teacher's role was to encourage self-expression rather than rote learning.

International Style Architectural style that developed in Europe in the 1920s and 1930s. The term was first used in 1932 by Henry-Russell Hitchcock and Philip Johnson. The style is characterized by rectangular forms, open interior spaces, the use of glass, steel and reinforced-concrete, with no decoration.

Modernism A late-nineteenth and twentieth century movement in all the arts, in which artists insisted on creating works that did not rely on previous historical models.

Organic architecture Frank Lloyd Wright's own term for an architecture that was harmonious within its parts and with its environment.

Pastiche Literally a medley or jumble, a work of art made up of fragments in the style of another artist.

Petroglyphs Rock carvings.

Pre-Colombian From the civilization in the Americas before the arrival of Columbus.

Quixotic Literally in the manner of Don Quixote. Figuratively, striving for lofty and visionary ideals.

Seditious From sedition, a concerted effort to overthrow a government.

Socialism A political theory advocating that land, property, capital and the means of production are owned jointly by the whole community.

Spanish mission Architectural style of the missions established by Spanish Franciscans in Florida, Texas, Arizona, New Mexico and California in the late-eighteenth and early-nineteenth centuries. Facades could be ornate, but the general effect was of simplicity.

Textile block Wright's own term for a concrete slab, created on site, imprinted with a pattern.

FURTHER READING

Books by Frank Lloyd Wright

An Autobiography, New York: Duell, Sloan and Pierce, 1932

Frank Lloyd Wright Collected Writings, Bruce Brooks Pfieffer (ed), Volumes 1–5, New York: Rizzolo, 1992–5

Frank Lloyd Wright: Writings and Buildings, Kaufmann & Raeburn (eds), New York: Horizon, 1960

The Future of Architecture, New York: Horizon, 1953

Genius and the Mobocracy, New York: Duell, Sloan and Pierce, 1949

The Living City, New York: Horizon, 1958

Modern Architecture: Being the Kahn Lectures for 1930, Carbondale: Southern Illinois University Press, 1987

The Natural House, New York: Horizon, 1954

A Testament, New York: Bramhall House, 1957

Books about Frank Lloyd Wright, his life and his buildings

Blake, *Peter, Frank Lloyd Wright: Architecture and Space*, Harmondsworth: Penguin, 1964

Blake, Peter, *No Place Like Utopia: Modern Architecture and the Company We Kept*, New York: Knopf, 1993

Constantino, Maria, *Frank Lloyd Wright*, New York: Crescent Books, 1991

DeLong, David G, (ed.) *Frank Lloyd Wright: Designs For An American Landscape, 1922–1932*, New York: Abrams, 1996.

Gill, Brendan, *Many Masks: A Life of Frank Lloyd Wright*, New York: Putnam's, 1987

Guerrero, Pedro E, *Picturing Wright: An Album From Frank Lloyd Wright's Photographer*, San Francisco: Pomegranate Artbooks, 1994

Lind, Carla, *Lost Wright: Frank Lloyd Wright's Vanished Masterpieces*, New York: Simon and Schuster, 1996

Lucas, Suzette A, *Taliesin West, In The Realm of Ideas*, Scottsdale: Frank Lloyd Wright Foundation, 1993

McCarter, Robert, *Frank Lloyd Wright*, London: Phaidon,1997

Pfeiffer, Bruce Brooks, *Frank Lloyd Wright*, Koln; Taschen, 1991

Pfeiffer, Bruce Brooks, *Frank Lloyd Wright in the Realm of Ideas*, Carbondale: South Illinois University Press, 1988

Pfeiffer, Bruce Brooks, *Frank Lloyd Wright: The Masterworks*, New York: Rizzoli, 1993

Sanderson, Arlene, *Wright Sites: A Guide to Frank Lloyd Wright Public Places*, Washington: Preservation Press, 1991

Scully, Vincent, *Masters of World Architecture: Frank Lloyd Wright*, New York: George Brazillier, 1990

Secrest, Meryle, *Frank Lloyd Wright: A Biography*, New York: Knopf, 1992

Smith, Kathryn, *Frank Lloyd Wright's Taliesin and Taliesin West*, New York: Abrams, 1997

Storrer, William Allin, *The Architecture of Frank Lloyd Wright: A Complete Catalogue*, Cambridge: MIT Press, 1978

Sweeney, Robert L, *Wright in Hollywood: Visions of a New Architecture*, Cambridge: MIT Press, 1994

Tafel, Edgar, *Years with Frank Lloyd Wright: Apprentice to Genius*, New York: Dover Publications, 1985

Wolfe, Tom, *From Bauhaus to Our House*, New York: Farrar Strauss Giroux, 1981

Wright, Olgivanna, *Our House*, New York: Horizon Press, 1959

Wright, Olgivanna, *Frank Lloyd Wright, His Life, His Works, His Words*, New York: Horizon, 1966

Wright, Olgivanna, *The Shining Brow: Frank Lloyd Wright*, New York: Horizon, 1960

INDEX

A Beginner's Guide

Other titles available in the Beginner's Guides Key Figures series: